London Living

Research and photographic co-ordination:
Anna Davenport
Designed by: Mark Vernon-Jones
Endpapers by: Lawrence Mynott
Typeset in: Didot

First published in the United States in 1997 by
Watson-Guptill Publications, a division of
BPI Communications, Inc.,
1515 Broadway, NY 10036

First Published in Great Britain in 1997 by
George Weidenfeld & Nicolson Ltd

Library of Congress Catalog Card Number: 97–061390
ISBN 0-8230-836-4
Printed and bound in Italy
1 2 3 4 5 6 7 8 9 10 / 06 05 04 03 02 01 00 99 98 97

London Living

LISA LOVATT-SMITH

Introduction by Paul Duncan

Whitney Library of Design
An imprint of Watson-Guptill Publications / New York

contents

There is no place like London. Its oddest characteristic – the one that sets it apart from other European cities – is its scattered, almost ad hoc, quality. Huge and sprawling, it's a place in which a collection of villages, real and imagined, historic and modern, is held loosely together by highways and bridges, crescents and squares and by the River Thames, which pushes its way through the city's centre. This books picks out interiors from across its spectrum. In London, people tend to inhabit houses, many with their own gardens. It may only be a patch at the front and back, but it's a garden nonetheless and its existence bestows a peculiar character on the city. Mostly low-rise, comparisons of London with other European cities in which, overwhelmingly, people live tightly packed into blocks of apartments, are revealing. On the Continent there is less greenery, far fewer parks and gardens, and less visible expanses of open sky. Shops and houses intermingle, if not in the same building, then in the same street. Not so in London. London, the old adage has it, is a 'collection of villages'. Some, like Marylebone, have medieval beginnings. Others are Georgian,

Introduction

by Paul Duncan

Regency or Victorian. Some are a mix, and today include an eccentric and eclectic collection of different building types. That's the romance of this metropolis. Many retain at their core the features of an earlier identity. Old Clapham is one, Hampstead another. In spite of its inherent tattiness, it is still possible to see in Clapham the last vestiges of a high street lined with buildings of differing ages, the remnants of a village green, a spire-adorned parish church, a churchyard filled with battered tombs and old roses, clusters of period houses (in this case Georgian) and a local 'big house'. They are tangible reminders of a forgotten world in another so different. In the north of the metropolis, Hampstead is still essentially a Georgian village, with cobbled lanes and old railings. The heath separating it from Highgate reinforces its appeal. Barnes retains its original duck pond, and Ham a fine, early seventeenth-century manor. Richmond, a village that took its name from the palace that King Henry VII built there in 1500, is dotted with early eighteenth-century houses. Many survive near the Thames, and close to Richmond Hill,

and the classic view of the river from the top of that hill – the one painted by numerous landscape artists – remains largely unspoilt, even now. Across London street names conjure up images of a lost rural world – Chelsea Manor Street (Chelsea), Millfield Lane (Highgate), Ladbroke Grove (Holland Park), The Chase (Clapham), and so on. Across London, and throughout the centuries, the villages grew, and were crystallized into towns and boroughs as the fields and meadows around them were developed by landowners and speculators. Piecemeal development ensured a disparity of design from one area to the next, and today the 'separateness' of these villages is marked, not only by their historical uniqueness, but also by the architectural characteristics of their buildings – their design, brickwork and pointing, stonework, ornamentation, doorcases, fenestration, metalwork, moulding details and overall urban texture. And so most of London's neighbourhoods have a clear and distinct identity. Cross a street separating neighbourhoods, and time after time you move from one world into another. Often Londoners can tell where they are by

London; a nation, not a city

(Disraeli)

London is a modern Babylon

(Disraeli)

the look of the surroundings through which they happen to be passing. Take Belgravia and Kensington. The over-whelming grandeur of the former's cream and bleached-white stucco terraced mansions, with their porticoed entrances, is at odds with the infinitely less terrifying proportions of Kensington's smaller brick or stucco villas, and tall, often gabled, nineteenth-century terraced houses. The streets are mostly wide and spacious in Belgravia, and are narrower in Kensington, where the public and private gardens are more prolific. There are grids of dignified Georgian brick terraces in Bloomsbury and Hampstead, and huddles of brightly painted cottages in Chelsea, while row after row of 1930s semi-detached houses in Shepherd's Bush herald the search for the suburban idyll. Texture – character, scale, materials and the relationship of buildings to greenery – marks each 'village' and makes it special. Londoners choose where to live accordingly, provided that the price is right. London's 'villages' are also marked by their individual social flavour. Traditionally, that's always been the case. Often, areas continue to be inhabited by those for whom neighbourhoods first were developed. Belgravia, once the home of aristocrats and plutocrats, retains its flavour through the embassies which have replaced them. The former residents have debunked to Kensington and Chelsea, once anything but affluent. In fact, the brightly painted cottages around Chelsea's Old Church Street, in reality hardly much more than two up-two downs in which artisans once lived, now change hands for hugely inflated prices. Hampstead is the home of intellectuals, and Camden Town the seat of self-conscious radicals. Notting Hill Gate and Ladbroke Grove, in the 1950s the ghettos of black immigrants, are now hotbeds of chic, while Bethnal Green, Bow, and other east London neighbourhood 'hamlets' mostly retain their traditional working-class residents, perhaps uniquely in inner London. Of course, these are not hard-and-fast rules – as this book shows. In fact, Londoners are nothing if not individual, and many of the homes included in this book are lived in by people who are at social odds with their neighbours. Painter Ricardo Cinalli's dark worker's cottage looks like any

The chief advantage of London is, that

a man is always so near his burrow

(Hugo Meynell)

London, that great cesspool into which all the

loungers of the Empire are irresistibly drained

(Arthur Conan Doyle, A Study in Scarlet*)*

other in Spitalfields. Inside, it's quite different. There it's a world dominated by sensual paint effects, and by a large glass pyramid-topped studio in which he works. Tiggy Maconochie and Aaron Budnik's apartment in Battersea would be like any other in the street if it weren't for the fact that her plain, turn-of-the-century room is dominated by a huge, roughly finished, wooden tardis-like structure, which provides multi-purpose accommodation in what was actually a recording studio. At Oriel Harwood and Stephen Calloway's home in deeply unfashionable Walworth, a rich feast of colour and texture is the main ingredient of rooms which are totally at odds with a bland exterior. And constant aesthetic change is the hallmark of an apartment in which living and working are inseparable. At David Gill's home, in Kensington, although the simple modernism of his rooms emulates the quiet classicism of his apartment's exterior, part of a nineteenth-century stuccoed house, there isn't much that hints at the bourgeois style that once enriched such a building's interior. That's what makes it so exciting. Most cutting edge of all, though,

And dream of London, small and white and clean,

The clear Thames bordered by its gardens green.

(William Morris, The Wanderers, *Prologue)*

London is the epitome of our times,

and the Rome of today

(Ralph Waldo Emerson, English Traits)

is John Young's radical conversion of a riverside apartment in Hammersmith. Sober and classical on the outside, and identical to many of the 1970s blocks on the adjacent plots, within a controlled anarchy has reduced the original rooms to just one space, which is light, airy and bold. The raw industrial materials used, and the delicate, high-tech features, like suspended staircases, make it a far cry from the terraced houses and the chintz of that particular neighbourhood's other exteriors and interiors. Most of the interiors shown in this book exhibit a successful mix of rationality and waywardness in their style and content. Perhaps that's the essence of Englishness, of living in London. The result is always highly personal, whether it's the home of a grandee, a writer, a decorator, a collector, or anyone else. Eccentric, mad, urbane, cool, elegant, witty, overblown – these are all worlds to which this book provides an introduction. The home is at the centre of any Londoner's existence. Home is where nearly all the entertaining takes place – not a particularly startling thought until you realize that in other places – Paris or Milan, say – the locals

socialize in restaurants. Daily life is often, though not exclusively, led 'locally'. Neighbours know each other. They meet in the streets and shop 'around the corner'. Rarely are houses and shops in the same street – traditionally, that's been the case since the nineteenth century. Compare this with Paris or Milan. In London, there is a neighbourhood street of shops, busy during the day but quieter at night, and at least two restaurants and a pub, and this 'high street' is the centre of 'village' life. Fulham Road and the King's Road are good examples, so is Portobello Road in Notting Hill Gate. Surrounding the 'villages' are the private and public gardens which help to create an environment usually rare in a densely populated urban capital. There is the intimacy of the Chelsea Physic Garden, with its herbs and arbours; the privacy of Ladbroke Gardens which, like other neighbourhood gardens, is reserved for keyholders only – generally the residents of the surrounding houses. Plane trees line the streets, and there are also oaks, beeches and chestnuts. And separating the 'villages' are the huge open parks for which London is famous –

Hyde Park, Green Park, Regent's Park, Kensington Gardens, Hampstead Heath and many others. London is the world's greenest city. Together 'village' and park contrive to reassemble the rural idyll in a metropolitan context. What rural scene exists in the English countryside without a distant church spire or a cluster of mellow, russet-coloured buildings to enliven the view? Without the proximity of these parks, perhaps the 'villages' would lose their integrity, and thus much of their personae. The English delight in the idea of the rural idyll, and English landscape gardeners refuse to 'violate' nature, trying instead to retain its character while correcting and improving it. Where they can, even in the heart of the city, they contrive to bring it as close as possible to, if not into, their homes. Thus everywhere you find tree-filled squares (a British compromise – their gardens are neither public nor quite private), little private front and back gardens, roof terraces and balconies. To be able to have all of this, to be able live some-where countrified and still enjoy the benefits of metropolitan life, has enormous appeal. Londoners thrive on it.

When a man is tired of London,

he is tired of life; for there is in

London all that life can afford.

(Samuel Johnson)

Craigie — everyone calls him Craigie — lives in a Victorian terraced house on a triangular square that is almost like a quiet little green. The houses in front 'are special and listed', simple Georgian townhouses that give this corner of Lambeth an almost provincial air. Once inside the front door, however, the artist's magical dream world transports you into quite another dimension. Much of Craigie Aitchison's work expresses his enchantment with colour, the joy of simple things — flowers, pets, toys; it is thus not surprising to find that his walls are painted pink, or that the mantelpiece groans under a candid collection of the things he loves. Friends send Craigie pop-up paper flowers, plastic statues of Technicolor saints, ceramic clocks in gilt, patterned plates and assorted souvenir 'snow scenes'. These appeal to his his sense of humour, and to the props department in his mind that carefully keeps inspiring bits and pieces for future use in paintings. His work is the visual equivalent of the literature known as magical realism. Almost every object depicted exists somewhere in this Lambeth interior. It is as if Craigie lives inside one of his own

I

canvases; the curios and keepsakes are props; the walls are similar to the washes of colour in his painted backgrounds, and the extended family of Bedlington dogs which he has so often immortalized, are ranged up and down the stairs. It is a true eccentric's house, not one that has been designed as such. It has more to do with the fact of Craigie's imaginary world being so peculiar and unique that it has seeped out of his person, dripped off his paintbrush and reconstituted itself around him. He paints and lives with what he likes: tender, flamboyant toys, and statues and fairy lights. His biographer, Andrew Gibbon Williams, evokes Craigie's 'highly distinctive

self' which, in artistic terms, signifies a lack of 'stylistic borrowing'. His interior is just as unique: the result of the spontaneous and organic accumulation of favourite objects over the last twenty-five years. It's a brighter, nicer, warmer reality, and reminds one of art-dealer Helen Lessore's definition of Craigie as being 'truly Mediterranean'. There is only one thing missing — the canaries that Craigie so often painted, and that were a real feature of his world: 'I do wish I'd kept them, but I suddenly got a real thing about keeping them in cages …' His three over-affectionate Bedlingtons do their best to make up for this loss. They 'live to be made a fuss of', and accompany him up and down the four-storey house, from the pink-and-red basement kitchen to the blue-and-white top-floor studio. On the turquoise studio floor an impressive pile of tortured, half-empty tubes of paint, and dirty brushes are a silent monument to Craigie's self-critical painting sessions. He sleeps next door, in a child's white wooden bed, with a canopy that a friend made for him. Throughout the house are assorted pieces of 'good' furniture, heirlooms from his family — his father was an eminent Scottish advocate. Their delicate lines, their gilt and carving work rather well with the 'rubbish, that just accumulates … you buy something to paint and it just stays there forever'.

Craigie Aitchison

On the previous pages: Craigie Aitchison and one of his Bedlington terriers in front of his Kennington home. The kitchen, in Craigie's favourite dusty pink, features an accumulation of kitschy objects, including a light shade in the form of a drum decorated with Scottish soldiers. *Above*: the living room with its patterned wallpaper and its Scotty-dog electric fire; the detail, *right*, shows a *naïf* religious print over the bedroom mantelpiece. *On the opposite page*: another view of the sitting room and its grandfather clock, a family heirloom. The smaller pictures show other fireplaces, all decorated as domestic shrines – the visual anchors of most of Craigie's rooms.

Ron Arad lives with his wife and two children in leafy Belsize Park, on the ground floor of an imposing house that hints at a well-ordered family life and comfortable interiors, and appears to be a million miles away from Arad's signature creations in cast iron and raw steel. As a designer, Israeli-born Arad is among Britain's most gutsy, working in materials that are still considered unsuitable for the domestic interior. Industrial textures, crudely bent metal, raw cement, dislocated car seats and ruinisim are a few of the tough features that Arad has brought into his clients' homes. The allure of metal screeching as it becomes exquisite furniture, bent, banged and twisted into improbable shapes, is less of a compulsion nowadays: during the 1990s, Arad has branched out into smoother, more sophisticated products. He can still handle a blowtorch with the best of them, however, and his brilliantly designed office has a metal workroom in which Arad spends most of his mornings. 'London living ... getting up in the morning, dropping the kids at school, coming here ...' Arad sits on one of his function-defying, comfortable, big chairs

2

made of the flat sheet metal that they would instantly revert to if you unscrewed the bolts. His deadpan humour is possibly the most constant element in his designs, as in his conversation. 'When I first came here to study at the Architectural Association, I had a preconceived idea of London that came from films and books. I didn't find that London of course, but I found something else. London is a vacuum. Living spaces are already perfectly defined: a chimney breast in every room, slanting storage under the stairs, a skirting board so that the vacuum cleaner doesn't leave marks on the walls, three up and two down. People have a set idea of how they want to live. Little garden on the street, big garden hidden away behind — the Victorians and Edwardians invented all that, and it is never questioned. The fact of this generalized indifference to design is precisely why it's a good place to live.' In his own 'English dream' of a home, Arad has done surprisingly little in the way of interior architecture. 'It's so classically good the way it is that it was not worth transforming. My ideal would be to live in a contemporary house, to design my own — but there isn't much of that in London.' Arad and his family have the basement, ground floor and garden of the original Edwardian house. He knocked the ground floor into one large room, which benefits from two big bay windows. As he has a deep-rooted aversion to curtains and all forms of blinds, he installed panes of sanded glass in the windows that face the road, 'translucent rather than transparent'. This is the only high-tech touch about the place — even the original cornices have been left untouched. The walls are Pompeian red in what used to be the front room and is now a television lounge. Most family life goes on in the unconvential kitchen which Arad installed in the main living space. Here the walls have been stained a deep sienna by applying wet pigments straight onto the plaster, and then waxing the surface. The cooking and preparing of food is done on a 'kitchen island', with curvy, shiny, aluminium surfaces. These amoeba-like shapes inspired Arad to create an installation of large, sinuous tables in reflecting aluminium for the opening of the Cartier Foundation in Paris. One of these tables, rather pleasingly, returned to London, and was promptly installed in the kitchen where the idea had originated. It is flanked by red-and-black original Arne Jacobsen chairs, 'picked up at markets and charity shops'. Over the table hangs a chandelier by Arad's friend Ingo Maurer. It is eloquently surreal, a vivid explosion of crockery and cutlery that lights the puzzle of a conventional room full of fantastically original furniture.

Ron Arad

On the previous pages: a portrait by Roland Beaufre of Ron Arad in his famous sheet-metal 'Big Chair', and a detail of the kitchen/dining room in his Belsize Park home; the sinuous, stainless-steel, mirror-polished table was designed by Arad in 1994, and reflects an antique wood cupboard of the kind often found in locker rooms: the Arads use it to store kitchenware. *Opposite*: Ron Arad's desk in a corner of the open-plan kitchen/dining room; the bookcase is his own 'Bookworm' design for Kartel, and the vintage chairs by designer Jacobsen were lucky market finds. *Above right*: Arad's 'Lovely Rita' shelving system, also for Kartel, used for spices and kitchen utensils.

Above: a detail of the mantelpiece in the living room showing a vase of Arad's design for Rosenthal. *Right*: a sofa from the early 1970s flanked by two tables made from old dartboards mounted on wrought-iron sewing-machine stands. The 'Tree Light', shaded bulbs on long, flexible tubing, is one of Arad's early designs from 1983. *Opposite*: another view of the living room, featuring one of the famous 'Rover' chairs designed by Arad in 1981 for his One-Off Gallery; the painting is by Gabriel Kalsmer, depicting abstract images punctured by large circles. Over the fireplace hangs a rusty, barbed-wire security panel; the light is by Igno Maurer, the piano stool on the right was also made by Arad, from a sewing-machine base.

Treating home as a squat, and going several degrees shabbier than shabby chic may not be everyone's idea of how to transform a crumbling London house, but then fashion designer Liza Bruce and furniture designer Nicholas Alvis Vega have never been terribly interested in conventional behaviour. They met at Holland Park School in the early 1970s, when Liza was just fourteen and, despite her father spiriting her off to a convent school in Mexico, Alvis Vega persevered and followed her. Youthful ardour, and a staunch belief in the better kinds of fairy tales, proved a match for parental disapproval, and ever since they have concentrated on creating a surreal masterpiece of their life. A best-selling but, 'madly inaccurate', cookbook was followed by a stint as vegetarian restaurateurs in California. A trip to Mustique, where 'I had nothing to wear', inspired Liza to become a swimwear designer, partly in order to fund Nicholas's artistic career. A successful spell in New York was followed by a return to London, where Alvis Vega has had several exhibitions. Their early Victorian house in Shepherd's Bush ended up being so much of a statement

3

that not only did the neighbours turn their noses up at it, but the bank manager panicked — after months of decorating and hard work the couple received a letter stating that he considered the house to be hovering on the brink of total abandon! Liza and Nicholas take it in turns to talk. 'I have always found derelict buildings to be really beautiful ... the house was like a setting for dreams of sleeping princesses and other mysteries.' 'We liked the idea of people passing by stopping to wonder who was living there, part of the interest of the house was to stimulate the imagination.' Unfortunately the princess' palace also stimulated two worrying robberies: 'We woke up one night and found a man standing right next to the bed.' Furthermore, as the apprehensive bank manager could not be converted to the cause of peeling paint, window panes covered in a glaze of violet emulsion, or the garden-as-a-wilderness concept, they recently ended up moving. Their home owed something to Beuys — a health-defying Louis xv-style sofa 'upholstered' in lead — and a lot to the Dadaist creed, recalling poet Tristan Tzara's famous 'Dada: the interweaving of contraries and of all contradictions'. The kooky aesthetics may be more Addams Family than Adams, but each corner of the house was a tableau, and somehow profoundly satisfying to the artist's eye, however unlikely the juxtaposition of decorative elements. This, Liza remarked, was the reaction to 'living in a huge, shapeless loft in Manhattan. Here we created little theatre sets in every tiny room'. Following a rolled-lead carpet up the unpainted stairs, the house was revealed as a unique combination of hard-core creative salvage and neo-classical decorative gestures. The floors were stained exactly the right shade of brown with coffee and Guinness. The rather grand mirror was left in its packing case. The curtains were draped, but only one was an Aubusson, the other being canvas. Dainty, gilded, Swedish eighteenth-century chairs ringed a stone garden table in the dining room, which had stripped-down walls revealing several generations' worth of peeling paint. The pipes were on view, and log fires threw out heat from a fireplace made of an assemblage of cast iron and hugely contrasting delicately carved wood. Flamboyant flowers were quite often shown either half dead and dropping petals, or pristine, still in their box and crackling with synthetic packaging. Bruce and Alvis Vega created a world of curious symbolism that overflowed with decorative ideas. Unconventional objects popped up everywhere, but as your eyes adjusted to the appearance of chaos, it became evident that, despite appearances, telephone and lighting all worked. 'It questioned the notion of beauty and comfort, but not the function – only form.'

Liza Bruce &
Nicholas Alvis Vega

On the previous pages: a portrait of the couple, and the overgrown façade of their home in Shepherd's Bush. *Left*: a view of the dining-room table in the ground-floor room in which the paint has been left to crumble, stripped back to the original plaster to serve as a visual reminder of the different decorative incarnations of the house; even the raw bricks of the mantelpiece become a decorative feature. The floorboards have been stripped, and the windows painted with violet emulsion so that the light that seeps through has an unreal quality to it.

Above: a corner of the kitchen; the sash window looks out onto the deliciously decadent and overgrown garden which caused the neighbours to complain; the perforated-metal screen was designed by Nicholas Alvis Vega; the floor has been dyed dark brown with a mixture of coffee and Guinness rubbed into the grain of the wood. *Right*: a detail of the shelving in the kitchen. The shelves have been lined and edged with ageing newspaper, in keeping with the shabby chic aesthetic favoured by the couple. *On the following pages*: the bathroom, with its early nineteenth-century iron tub; the window is draped with a gold-thread sari, and the chair was designed by Alvis Vega

Opposite: a *tableau* of dead and dying flowers placed in a series of wooden boxes. The detail, *left*, shows the sink made from a giant seashell in a small washroom. *Below*: the iron bed in the loft, with its sloping ceiling and peeling paint. As in other parts of the house, there is a collection of fragments of prettily carved wood. This apparently unkempt effect was 'much more hard work than doing the house up the conventional way', in the words of Alvis Vega.

Ian Chee is a young Singaporean pianist-turned-architect, who gets a lot of curious passers-by staring through his ground-floor windows – transfixed by the sight of a gaudy Andy Warhol hung over the mantelpiece. The wicked truth, however, is that the ultra-recognizable Marilyn is not what it seems, but rather a poster salvaged from a hoarding. This light-hearted attitude towards art, collecting, and all the pomposity that they so often represent, is typical of Chee's interior. His small, high-ceilinged pad looks like an expensive designer scheme, with much thought and endless funds poured into a careful, almost too careful, selection of fine 1950s furniture, but the truth is that it was all done by Chee and his associate — on a budget so modest that they won't even discuss it. The garden flat is good example of imagination replacing purchasing power, and is much to the advantage of the project and its inspiring spatial juxtapositions. Chee left Singapore to study fashion, and although he was accepted at that Mecca of style, St Martin's School of Art, he soon decided that frocks and furbelows were not for him, and that he

4

would rather launch himself into a career in architecture. He ended up at the Architectural Association, 'because they were the only school still interviewing a week before the start of term'. It was a decision he never regretted, and he has since started up his own company, VX designs. His flat was renovated on a shoestring budget when his design company was still at the stage of being based in his spare room. 'I had been flat-hunting for a long time, and not only in Kensington. It could have been anywhere really. I was looking for a derelict space, which despite the elegant address this very nearly was … it was the annex to the main house, and originally the ballroom. It had a partition across the main space and quite a lot of work had to be done to expose the original proportions. There was no electricity, no heating and no water, except for a sink in the middle of the room. I recreated the fireplaces, installed a kitchen, removed two walls, changed the floorboards in the corridor, reopened a skylight, opened up a window in the rear, and then painted it all white because white emulsion was the cheapest.' Chee invested in low-cost staples, like the linoleum in the kitchen, but chose a speckly variety that would give a more interesting effect. Ordinary white chipboard was used for the kitchen cupboards, but he had the wall tiles specially made out of terrazzo studded with glittering fragments of marble, mirror and old blue glass from bottles that he had collected. The garden had to wait a year but, feeling that landscaping was not his forte, Chee allowed himself the small extravagance of calling in 'someone who would do it properly first time round'. John Paul Fraser collaborated on the 'Zen' pebble-and-concrete-tiles affair on Chee's tiny plot, that required minimum maintenance. It also had the effect of continuing the same quirky aesthetic that prevails in the interior, which is furnished with brightly coloured, twentieth-century design classics. Chee shrugs off his wonderful collection of designer furniture with the same irreverence he had when hanging his 'Warhol'. 'They have all been picked up at flea markets and in skips … I am an architect and not a decorator, so I am naturally attracted to this kind of design, as the furniture can be seen as a collection of sculptures rooted in space. The pieces have to work as objects, and they have to work with the Steinway – that's the only criteria.'

Ian Chee

On the previous pages: a portrait of Chee, his associate Voon Wong, and a view of his Zen garden at the back of his Kensington home. *Opposite*: a view out of the kitchen window showing the breakfast table and the bar stools from Camden. *Above*: the large, ground-floor flat has harmonious proportions which enabled Chee to house his grand piano and his collection of vintage design pieces with ease: the Danish day bed and the Ottoman by Noguchi. *Right*: the dining table by A. J. Milne, with its classic chairs in bright plastic by Panton.

Opposite: the chimney breast was reduced to a 'hole in the wall' to suit Chee's modernistic approach to his nineteenth-century interior. The Marilyn Monroe screen print by Warhol is, in fact, a poster rescued from a billboard. Passers-by often gaze at it through Chee's ground-floor window, obviously thinking that it is the genuine article. On the cowskin rug is a table by Habitat, and to the left a chair by Jacobsen, another contemporary design icon. The surprising thing about this interior is that nearly all of the classic twentieth-century pieces were picked up for next to nothing at markets in London and Paris. *Above*: a view of Chee's study, which has been cleverly worked out to include lots of storage space.

Ricardo Cinalli is an Argentinian painter who first arrived in England in 1974, 'at the tail end of the hippy movement'. He had just completed a degree in psychology at Rosario University. He remembers with amusement that London seemed to have turned punk, 'which did not attract me in the least. It is just not part of the Latin culture — I mean have you ever seen a *South American* punk?' London gave him the necessary impetus seriously to consider becoming a painter and when a friend offered him studio space, he realized that his life had taken a definite direction. The studio in question turned out to be in a rather grand, early Georgian house in Spitalfields, which he then helped to restore. 'Spitalfields was wonderful then. In the whole of Fournier Street, which has now become very fashionable, there were only Gilbert and George, the vicar and us. The rest of the old houses were lived in by Bengalis … It had not yet become a conservation area, and the winos and the prostitutes used to light huge bonfires in the streets in winter and sprawl around them. It was like a scene out of Rembrandt.' It was at this point, and in order to decorate the

5

house, that Cinalli began to explore the world of Renaissance frescoes: the techniques he discovered, coupled with his impressive facility for drawing, led him to become a master of the decorative *trompe l'œil*. More significantly, the allegorical themes of classical iconography supplied him with the pictorial language that was to permeate most of his early paintings. In Fournier Street, he also began to create his characteristic large-scale works, which in their most frequent form are pastel drawings on layer upon layer of fine tissue paper. The superimposed images give an almost three-dimensional effect to the work, and produce interesting modifications to the colour and form. As his paintings got vaster — a drawing of a human ear would be man-sized — Cinalli regretfully decided to search for a new space. 'I was thinking of a warehouse; I'd had enough of the confined proportions of old Georgian buildings … but then I happened to visit a neighbouring house which was previously a dairy. It was near-derelict, but with an incredible view of the spire of the Hawksmoor church. That church seemed to act as a magnet, and suddenly I just could not bear the idea of leaving it…' So, for 'purely sentimental' reasons, Cinalli ended up in a 'tiny' four-storey house, with diminutive rooms, flimsy partitions, involving lots of building work — and a fabulous view. It was not entirely an act of impulse, however, because Cinalli had realized that as the building was not listed he could cover the garden and excavate under the house until he obtained his dreamed-of 'large, white studio'. It seemed a visionary, if somewhat ambitious, project. As skip after skip of earth was filled, and more and more Georgian bits and pieces — pipes, coins, china, hair rollers and human bones — emerged from the excavation, Cinalli fled to South America for a break, only to learn that storms had ravaged London, that Spitalfields was incommunicado, and that his house had most probably collapsed. Luckily, 'because it was sandwiched in the terrace', the house withstood the elements then as it had for almost 300 years. The studio finally began to take form, as a 'white cube', four metres (thirteen feet) below ground level, with a skylight that frames that fateful church spire. Under a square pane of resistant glass, the floor contains Cinalli's own 'Spitalfields museum', displaying the most interesting finds rescued during the digging work. Upstairs, the partitions have gone, and the interiors are warmer, either wood panelled or frescoed. 'Each floor has quite a different character, which is why I think of it as a schizophrenic house. Downstairs there is the space for creation: with the studio and the first floor *salon* where I play the piano; then come the spaces for ablutions, sleeping, eating. It's upside down in the nicest possible way. I always think of it as a tower capped by a blue "heaven" kitchen. The spirit of the house is quite romantic.'

Ricardo Cinalli

On the previous pages: a portrait of Cinalli, and the boarded-up shop front which is the ground-floor façade of his eighteenth-century Huguenot weaver's house in Spitalfields. *Left*: the first-floor living room, with its painted canvas carpet and the piano that Cinalli considers his domestic altar, loaded down with photographs, religious statuettes, sheet music and bowls of the brightly coloured pigments which he uses in his work; he mostly plays it during sessions with his Irish cleaning lady, who also happens to be a wonderful soprano. The panelling is original, and has been stripped and waxed. The artwork is all by Cinalli himself.

Above and right: views of the ingenious bedroom/bathroom on the second floor. Cinalli considers this room to be a three-dimensional artwork, an art installation in which chunks of plaster have been fixed to the wall and incorporated into a massive *trompe l'œil* on the theme of classical sculpture. The wooden floor has also been painted, and thus contributes to the overall effect. The amusing truth behind the matter is, of course, that Cinalli only hit upon the idea of a three-dimensional frieze on the wall when he found himself landed with plaster fragments from the demolition of the partitions on the first floor: 'it was much more fun to use sculpturally than to get rid of the debris'.

Right: a view of the kitchen on the top floor of the house. It is this room that boasts the splendid view of Spitalfields' Church, designed by Hawksmoor, with its distinctive spire which convinced Cinalli that he should buy the house. He now feels so attached to the church that he seriously questions if he will ever be able to live far from its shadow again. The kitchen was entirely painted in blue, green and white; his decorative scheme included the furniture, the floor and even the fridge. This playful theme was continued with a lively collage of photographs, postcards and invitations on the back of the kitchen door, and part of Cinalli's collection of nineteenth-century children's toys.

Above: a detail of the candelit kitchen. The chairs are all different, and are decorated with individual *trompe l'œil* motifs. *Right*: a view of the white cube of the sunken studio, excavated under what used to be the back garden. This mammoth task was instigated by Cinalli as the only solution to his pressing need for a skylit workspace. The myriad of bits and pieces evoking Spitalfields' richly historical past, unearthed during the excavation, have been conserved and set into the floor under glass – the painter calls it his very own Huguenot museum. On the wall hangs his massive artwork, *The Last Supper*, and in the foreground is an installation – composed of a laid table covered in the debris of a meal – on the same theme.

Ian Dew is one of those self-taught and instinctive designers who can put a house together out of architectural salvage, inventing new techniques as he goes along, and thoroughly enjoying the process. A veteran of a million car-boot sales, and with a wicked eye for the potential of any abandoned bit of wood or brick, he has no classic stylistic references to speak of, and only a theatrical imagination to thank for the inspiring interior of what was once a very ordinary house in deepest Streatham. Dew is very much his own man, but is aided and abetted by his ex-girlfriend, Alison Martin who is a specialist in paint finishes and *tromp l'œil.* It is worth recording that they met while she was picking up poles from a railway siding which she wanted to have made into a big, grand bed. Dew fervently believes that 'everyone should have their own special bed, made according to their fantasies', so their relationship developed from there. The darkly painted exterior is the first indication that the house is not quite like the others in the late Victorian terrace. The colour was inspired by the rich tones of Guinness, Dew's favourite drink. You can also guess at it being small

6

and tight inside, not an easy place to decorate, but Dew has somehow managed to open up a Technicolor world of possibilities, in which each room evokes a very different atmosphere. 'When I first discovered it, it was all done to bland, middle-of-the-road taste, what they call "builders finish" ... magnolia paint and white fitted cupboards. I wanted the complete opposite, somewhere that would be unique to live in. I believe that creating your own home, projecting your own spirit onto the design, is one of the few things that can make you really feel like an individual.' Dew dug down into the cellar to create a mystical red dining room under the stairs. He also did away with one of the spare bedrooms and the conventional bathroom to create a large, walk-in dressing room and shower, and his *pièce de résistance*, a Japanese-style bathroom in cedar shingles with a huge, wooden tub. 'Lifestyle is about experiencing pleasure, and a traditional Japanese tub which you can share with someone, float in, listen to music in ... spend your afternoon in, that's it.' Indeed, a window hung with strings of 'stained-glass' medallions, that glimmer on the water, adds to the hedonistic effect.

Dew sees himself as an 'urban Aboriginal caught in a high-tech lifestyle. It's so easy to forget that everything comes down to eating, sleeping, bathing and relaxation, and trying to do those things in the nicest possible way'. The beauty of the house lies in the finer touches. There are, for instance, three different types of wooden floor, delicately inlaid with either mosaic, slate or ceramic. The light sources have been carefully thought out 'to respect the flow of natural light'. The dragon tiles on the walls have been hand-moulded (from the carving on the back of a hairbrush); most of the door panels have been removed and replaced with stained glass. Experiments with textures and surfacing are in every room. Such is the incredible attention to detail that Dew considers to be vital to the life of the house and the 'pleasure zone' that it has become.

Ian Dew

Illustrating pages 54 and 55 are a portrait of Ian Dew, and a corner of the funky back garden, with its wooden table for eating al fresco. On page 56, there is a view of the lower-ground-floor dining room, painted a rich, distressed red. On page 57, the ground-floor study is a good example of how Dew manages to create intensely atmospheric rooms with the imaginative use of low-cost materials and furniture: the wall is covered in dyed and varnished chipboard, a tongue-in-cheek reference to the oak-panelled study. *Opposite*: the deep, Japanese-inspired wooden tub is the central piece in the bathroom, and the walls are covered in matching organic wooden 'tiling'. The stained-glass discs hanging in the window reflect their jewel-like colours onto the water, and add to the sensual pleasure of a long soak.

Opposite: the kitchen table is set into the bay window in a corner of this cleverly decorated room; the screen, with its cutouts and handprint motif, is a typically jokey piece of Dew's design. The details, *left and below*, show the kitchen counter, with its chessboard tile effect, and its clever, 'abacus' beaded cupboard doors. These sophisticated touches have given quite a different appearance to what was once a very ordinary kitchen.

Above: a mirror mosaic has been set into the wall of the spare bedroom, which is decorated in a Carribbean palette to evoke sunnier places. *Left*: the wall has been left bare, and the powdery distemper allows the texture of the bricks beneath to show through, adding to the southern feel. *Right*: in the master bedroom the bed has been created out of bits of old garden railing, as Dew is fond of making beds which are artworks, using the principles of creative salvage and his own, distinctly individual, artistic flair.

There is something quintessentially English about Christopher Gibbs' rooms at the Albany in Piccadilly. The place itself is a remnant of another age, 'the early nineteenth-century conversion by Henry Holland of the original 1770s building into chambers for gentlemen who had homes in the country and did not want the expenses and complications of a large London establishment ...' Such an institution could only exist in that particular slice of Westminster between Pall Mall and Conduit Street, and seems to have come straight out of Thackeray. It belongs to the world of exclusive clubs, such as White's or Brook's; evokes the traditional undergraduate rooms at Cambridge and Oxford; and improbably enough is lived in by Gibbs in the same spirit in which it was created. His real home is in Oxfordshire, and these rooms are simply convenient for work and other London pastimes. 'I only camp here really. I catch up with news, put up stray friends, and walk to work in my dressing gown if I want to. The Albany has the atmosphere of an Oxford college in the holidays — permanently.' Gibbs' antique shop, which is so grand that he can

7

only afford to have the odd piece on show, is situated at the corner of the Albany and Vigo Street. Nothing could be more pleasant, as walking to work involves a mere saunter through the Albany's arched colonnade, past the thermometer, 'which you can pretend to examine if you see someone coming from the other direction …' One of the many terribly English things about Gibbs is the lack of pomp or circumstance which surrounds the decoration of his two rooms. It is a classical bachelor's flat, with a large drawing room and a bedroom-cum-study, in which almost every piece of fabric or furniture is a collector's item, but in which all is arranged with a perfect disregard for what he terms 'swanking'. He claims not to have redecorated since 1975, when he reinstalled the fireplaces and laid the huge, old Axminster carpet to completely cover the floor. It is comfortable and lived in, not particularly tidy, but featuring interesting furniture and books that you really want to read on the shelves. The walls are decorated in a flamboyant, solid colour, evoking Gibbs' rock-and-roll past as a grand Chelsea hippy, and his long sojourns in Morocco, where he still spends much of his time. These escapades have also contributed to the particular mix of North African textiles and objects with pedigreed English antiques. 'Everyone has their own ingredients in their own soups. I don't fuss about these things … I like Classical Revival designs and Romantic objects. I like soft, painted, faded surfaces, and rich, shiny wooden things all mixed up. I like fossils and shells, and bits of classical sculpture about. Things that have lived.'

Christopher Gibbs

On the previous pages: a portrait of Gibbs, and a view from his
drawing room into the hall of his rooms at the Albany. As is
often the case with Gibbs' own interiors, his small London pad
is an inspired mix of North African objects and good English
furniture, overlaid with a selection of exotica. *Above*: a view of
Gibbs' bedroom, with his classical brass bed and adjoining
bathroom featuring a Victorian basin and an oval, eighteenth-
century mirror. The walls are decorated in a deep green that
adds to the club-like atmosphere. *Opposite*: a Regency
Axminster Turkish-style carpet, and a sofa of the same period
covered in linen and hand-painted to an eighteenth-century
Indian design, set the tone for the drawing room.

'One of the most fascinating contemporary artistic phenomena, an aesthetic partnership', thus are Gilbert and George described in the catalogue of one of their most recent exhibitions. The two artists have been working together since they first met at St Martin's School of Art in the 1960s. Although Gilbert is from the Dolomites, and George is from Devon, they come from similar, traditional, modest, country backgrounds. They both ended up at St Martin's more or less by accident, and began to work together, shocking other students and teachers alike with their ideas. At the core of their art was the concept of themselves *becoming* the art. Ever since their 1969 happening, when, gold-painted, they became 'singing sculptures', they have included themselves, or their images, in most of their pieces. In their inevitable, rigid, strangely timeless suits — identical, and always with all three buttons done up — their physical presence has intimately imposed itself on the collective unconscious of art. Spitalfields, where they have lived since 1964, is the framework to their lives. Its multi-racial community figures in their art; they lunch every day

8

at the same local 'caff'; they dine at neighbouring Indian restaurants. Their home, a distinguished, eighteenth-century Huguenot weaver's house, contains extraordinary collections of books, ceramics and Arts-and-Crafts furniture. 'When we first came here it was unbelievably cheap. The area was entirely Jewish, and the ancient Jewish landlords didn't mind you living in your studio.' 'As things evolved, the synagogue became a mosque, the Jews left, and the Maltese, then later the Bangladeshis took over.' Gilbert and George, veterans of a thousand triangular interviews, take it in turns to speak. For the interviewer it is vaguely reminiscent of a well-ordered tennis match, as the conversation flows naturally from one to the other artist. 'We started off with the ground floor and eventually bought the house in 1974. To get to the essence of the house was an enormous job. Originally it was to be painted, but by the time we had stripped down the panelling to the wood, we liked it so much that we decided to leave it that way. We waxed it all ourselves. We are not fanatics of the eighteenth century, or of historical authenticity. We just liked it that way.' 'Everybody who saw it empty said we mustn't put anything in it. It looked so beautiful empty. We just sat in two chairs we had from college, green.' 'We could have gone for tubular office furniture but we met Jeremy Cooper, a specialized London dealer, and started collecting Arts and Crafts.' 'We bought a lot, quickly, over about six years. Thousands of vases. A lot of things by Christopher Dresser.' 'And then we cut off very quickly.' In those six short years of discriminating and informed buying, the spirit of this unique interior was created: monumental, somehow impassive. A universe in waxed wood and ceramics; everything slightly out of proportion with the eighteenth-century rooms. By contrast, at the back of their house, spreading to encompass next door's garden, lie two ultra-modern studios in which the couple create their photographic pieces. This pristine, white, technical world is aeons away from the oiled 1790s panelling of the six-storey house. This juxtaposition evokes the stimulating contradiction apparent in the artists themselves: utterly modern in their techniques, and yet singularly old-fashioned in their daily living. At Gilbert and George's the telephone is frowned upon, the door is opened by a manservant, and an electric kettle serves as an excuse for a kitchen; they never eat in. All their collections are impeccably arranged, and the rooms appear as a series of still-life tableaux, almost like their work itself. They are creatures of habit, and their life is as ordered as the rare 1880s pottery that is lined up strictly on the massive, oversized wooden furniture. The lifestyle they have created is, in its antiquated simplicity and beauty, somehow almost as disturbing as their work.

Gilbert & George

On the previous pages: a previously unpublished portrait of Gilbert and George by Nick Knight, as well as a view of the exterior of their house. *Left and below*: the house is filled with a unique collection of Arts-and-Crafts furniture, and much of it is of Gothic inspiration, by designers such as Charles Eastlake, William Butterfield, Bruce Talbert and Augustus Pugin, among others. The plain wood of these imposing pieces is the perfect foil to vast collections of pottery from the 1880s, from such illustrious sources as the Brannan Art Pottery Works and Bentall. There is a special emphasis on the work of Christopher Dresser. Gilbert and George's collection is certainly one of the most important of its kind.

Above, below and right: further images of Gilbert and George's wood-panelled rooms, in which the accumulation of the pottery that they collect gives an unusual atmosphere to the house. The enamelled tones and fascinating design of the late nineteenth-century table and decorative ware are set off by bookshelves crammed with children's books of the same period, as well as a famed collection of vintage erotic literature with a homosexual theme.

When, at length, you do manage to penetrate to David Gill's immaculate Kensington quarters, it is abundantly clear that here lives a man of extremely sophisticated tastes. He apologizes for the mess — but there is no mess. No mess, no fuss, no rough edges, no errors of judgment. Just a soothing purity, an aesthetic's dream. The furniture is entirely composed of collector's items. A few choice pieces from the decorative arts of the 1930s and 1940s are matched with examples of the kind of modern design that Gill sells through his well-known London gallery. The atmosphere is curiously difficult to place, but then Gill has a cosmopolitan past, having being born in France and brought up in Spain. The artists whom he champions are often just as international, and the proof of the symbiotic relationship that he has with them is all over the flat. The table in the hall was made to measure by the design superstars Garouste & Bonetti, who were unknown in the United Kingdom when he met them. The textile designer who made his baroque cushions is now inundated with commissions (and is hopelessly expensive). A collection of

9

boxes on a side table are by Line Vautrin, a 1940s jewellery and object designer, who was living almost forgotten in Paris until Gill staged a show for her. Gill possesses a remarkable instinct in his choice of artists, which has served him well. 'I thrive on working with artists to bring out their creative spirit, their soul. It is a collaborative process. It provides them with a motivation if they know someone is going to bring their work forward.' Gill moved into the neo-classical terraced block overlooking a pretty garden square in the late 1980s. He immediately embarked on restructuring the space to transform the ordinary, two-bedroom flat into a fitting frame for the objects with which he wanted to live. As a consummate perfectionist, this involved laying a herringbone parquet floor with unusually wide slats, and staining, polishing and varnishing it a hundred times to simulate mahogany. It also took a number of trials to get the putty colour of the walls just right to provide the perfect foil for his extensive collection of Cocteau drawings and ceramics. 'You can hang anything on the walls now, and it works. They are the ideal neutral colour that changes with the light and gives a living quality to the room, neutral but not too much so.' The radiator covers, which in general are 'not very pleasing to the eye', were redesigned by Gill to simulate an architectural pattern. The curtains are two superimposed layers of silk in glowing gold and cream, so that the light may be 'warmed up at will'. A simple 1950s-style pelmet — once thought irretrievably unfashionable — was also designed, so that the curtains would convey that 'certain elegance' which is the trademark of the flat. Eliminating the mouldings has enhanced that impression further. In true bachelor fashion, the kitchen, with its specially designed cupboards in iron, is small and hidden away. The mirrored bathroom evokes the 1930s, as all the fittings were salvaged from the refurbishment of the Savoy Hotel. The entrance hall, with the bedroom off to the left and the living room to the right, doubles as a dining room when Gill entertains his artists, or fellow lovers of his other passion, the opera.

David Gill

On the previous pages: a portrait of David Gill, and a view of his living room and the L-shaped, early 1930s sofa designed by Eugène Printz, upholstered in a deep-purple velvet fabric by Manuel Canovas. Funnily enough, he had actually sold this sofa to a friend of his, and it was only upon moving in that he realized that he just had to have it back. The cushions are embroidered with 'rice stitch' by Ulrike Lilyedahl; the limed-oak table is a 1935 piece by Jean-Charles Moreux. The 1958 drawing is by Jean Cocteau, as are most of the ceramic plates in Gill's apartment. *Left*: the entry hall doubles as a dining room, and its centre piece is a table that he commissioned from designers Garouste & Bonetti; the chairs are 1930s pieces by André Arbus. *Below*: a view from the dining room, with its mirrored, folding doors leading into the small bedroom. Reflected in the doors is a 1960s artwork by Takis. *Right*: detail of the marble bathroom, with its 1930s fittings bought at the Savoy Hotel sale.

Within a certain London elite — those that used to seek out her Knightsbridge shop on the fifth floor of Harvey Nichols — Nathalie Hambro is known and revered as the epitome of chic. She is a maverick designer who has turned her hand to everything from stationery to publishing to tableware and fashion acessories. She has the knack of giving an unexpected twist to all she touches, from her 'cooking for the senses' to her hand-bound scrapbooks in multi-coloured papers. Her flat is a shifting stage for many of her eclectic creations. Nathalie Hambro has that slightly exotic allure and boyish sexiness that is unequivocally French; her home, however, has a type of eccentricity about it that is more English than Continental. Her large, classically Victorian flat in Pimlico is both studio and living space to her. It has a parallel role as an experimental testing ground for all things gastronomic, as Hambro is that rarest of all London creatures, the consummate cook and entertainer. 'All my design theories emanate from the flat. It is here that I usually adapt ideas picked up on my travels. It has a mysterious alchemy, being both a design laboratory and a refuge.' She is

10

inspired by the feathers, stones and other bits and pieces that she has found and collects and that are intricately arranged on tables and walls. Industrial elements have been turned into decorative gestures. Her love affair with metal — she wears chain-mail gloves and bags, has barbed-wire decorations in her kitchen and metal stencils on her walls — is an intimate affair stemming from a childhood fascination with hardware shops and nuts and bolts. 'Home is a synthesis of the things I love, and it is adapted to the slightly self-centred way I live. I don't need much sleep, for instance, so there is no proper bedroom. Instead all the rooms are multi-functional. The Hambro penchant for moving furniture around in the middle of the night means that the flat is in a permanent state of evolution. 'The layout of the 1880s building is wonderful. It is very spacious but funnily enough people tend to crowd out the smallish kitchen. I love to cook in front of guests, experimenting with recipes.' She describes herself as 'curious, investigative, obssesive', mixing flavours and ingredients from different cultures with impunity. There is much more to her than gastronomic virturosity, however. There is the erudite streak that inspires her to hold a literary *salon* in her drawing room as befits her studies at the Ecole du Louvre in her native Paris. She is well read, in the nineteenth-century sense of the word: poetry, psychology, the esoteric arts, and literature for literature's sake. Then there is the particularly English fascination with fancy dress and theatricals, which has inspired many an uproarious party, and even the commissions to organize fundraising fancy-dress balls for the Royal Academy and the British Museum. Most intriguing of all there is the boundless curiosity and impressive energy that is packed into that lithe, sophisticated frame, and that compelled her to leave her London life behind her for months and go travelling *alone* all over India, Laos, and Thailand. Such is the nature of this multi-cultural adventurer whose own favourite description of her world is: 'East meets West, the opulence of the East with the modernity of the West.'

Nathalie Hambro

On the previous pages: a portrait of Nathalie Hambro, and the façade of the classical Pimlico terrace in which she lives, overlooking one of those communal squares for which London is famous. *Opposite*: a view of the kitchen in which Nathalie Hambro spends much of her time concocting new delicacies for the cookbooks that she writes. The aluminum and gunmetal fixtures reflect Hambro's love of all things metallic. *Above right*: a detail of her old-fashioned kitchen stove, and of the impressive battery of kitchen utensils from all over the world.

Left: a view of the 'celestial' bathroom, painted deep blue. The basin is set into a nineteenth-century chest of drawers in mahogany. *Right*: the striped walls of a multi-purpose study/dining room add warmth to a room in which reading and dressing-up are favourite activities; the latter inspired by the antique costumes which Hambro collects, they hang on the walls as three-dimensional works of art, such as the nineteenth-century *toreros* costume found in Nîmes (far right). The bed, in cast iron, is French, and the wallpaper panel behind is an example of nineteenth-century découpage; the garden table and chairs add to the informal atmosphere that prevails in the apartment.

Left: a view of the Chinese-imperial-yellow living room, with its bookshelves and mahogany William IV *chaise longue* evoking that nineteenth-century gentlewoman's pastime of which Hambro is an enthusiast, the *salon literaire*. The heavy wooden mirror was originally part of a mantelpiece, and was found in a junk shop. The bench in the foreground is also William IV. *Above*: a detail showing some metal stars by Tom Dixon, and a chicken-wire sculpture created *en lieu* of a Christmas tree by Hambro; it is also decorated with stars.

The *tout-Londres* had hardly become aware of the overnight romance between the potter Oriel Harwood and the collector and decorative-arts scholar Stephen Calloway before they were engaged and house-hunting. The marriage of two such great aesthetes boded well for the exuberance of the conjugal home, and indeed they were not to disappoint. Satisfying Calloway's desire for an old house and Harwood's for a more neutral space, they compromised, and moved into a large Georgian house in deeply unfashionable Walworth that had been stripped of almost all its original features. Thus it had the right classical proportions, but not too much of an intrusive historical presence to detract from the very personal atmosphere that they were bound to bestow upon it. Calloway has been collecting since the age of fourteen, an activity which he then financed by painting after school during the week, selling his efforts on Saturday mornings prior to disappearing down the Portobello Road to look for bargains. Ensconced in the Victoria and Albert Museum, where he advises on all sorts of related matters, he is steeped in the history of

II

decoration. He has written ten books on the subject, and describes himself as an admirer of Horace Walpole, that eighteenth-century writer and wit-about-town who wrote of his own house as his 'little play-thing'. This is a succinct eulogy for the approach that has transformed 'Otranto House' (after Walpole's first 'Gothick' novel, *The Castle of Otranto*) into 'the most elaborate and entertaining game imaginable'. The Calloways did not want anything too strict or too nostalgic, and did not want a house to serve as a museum for their collections; most important of all, they wanted to have fun. In Harwood's words: 'We saw the house as a kind of dressing-up box.' Both had to have their own space: a basement studio for Harwood, where she works at what Stephen calls her 'blobby home-made pottery'; a study — he calls it the library — for him, in his preferred dark and dramatic mode, with the contents of his ninety crates of books and objects about him. 'The interiors Stephen makes up always depend on the grouping of objects for their effect', says Harwood. 'I sometimes feel the necessity of my work being seen in something other than an antique context. As I like complex forms, they are forever being automatically referenced to the past, whereas there are lots of things I make that are not about the past at all.' The finished house is about an 'interweaving of the old and the new', about a merging of their two worlds, about the bizarre and the baroque, about great English eccentric decorating schemes leavened with a dose of seventeenth-century Spanish influence and some flowery Sicilian pastiche. They can, of course, practice irreverence all the better because they are true connoisseurs: curtains made for Napoleon III's visit to Windsor are held back by gilded steak tenderizers; a candle-holder is magicked from a towel rail; true antiquities rub shoulders with plaster casts ... A lilac-and-green, yellow-and-red cacophony of colours dominates the drawing room, inspired by the excesses of Brighton Pavilion, and by Harwood's *Snakes* chimney piece. On the ground floor, room has even been found for a seventeenth-century curiosity cabinet, inspired by the German *Wunderkammer.* Here corals, bones, shells, books and fossils – some old, some new, some valuable, some not, are exposed side by side. Like the rest of the house, it is a very personal ode to the ridiculous and to the sublime, all deeply theatrical, but very modern in its relaxed appreciation of such juxtapositions. Beauty is the only criteria. Indeed, William Morris' statement, 'Have nothing in your homes that you do not know to be useful or believe to be beautiful' expresses Calloway's sensibility to perfection. They enjoy their house, 'decorated terribly economically, and grubby but delightful', as few people do, and every moment of their shared lives reflects the sense of fun that has shaped their glamorous decorating schemes.

Oriel Harwood & Stephen Calloway

On the previous pages: portraits of Harwood and Calloway, and a view of the luxuriant back garden which was one of the decisive factors in their choosing to move into this large Walworth house. *Opposite*: a view of the flamboyant Chinoiserie drawing room conceived around some of Harwood's large degree-show ceramic pieces; the snake motif she adopted inspired the couple to create an oriental effect. *Above*: Calloway's book-lined study filled with some of his favourite objects. This room is inspired by the homes of celebrated eighteenth- and nineteenth-century collectors of sculpture, paintings and idiosyncratic *objets d'art*.

Above: the canopied bed in the romantic, candlelit bedroom in which a fire is always kept burning in winter. The couple's collection of books has spilt over into even this intimate space. *Top right*: the bathroom, with its old-fashioned boxed bath and theatrical furnishings. *Below right*: an ingenious photograph of the stairwell, lined with fragments of sculptures, plaster casts and prints, which once again evokes the admiration that Calloway has for such great British collectors of the past as Lord Leighton, Sir William Hamilton and Sir John Soane.

More has been written about this 'iceberg' in Islington than about almost any other contemporary London family home. On first view, it appears to have been built entirely of glass, a futuristic Roald Dahl-like exercise in make believe that has mistakenly landed in deepest N1 among the more mundane Georgian semis that make up the neighbourhood. It was the result of an inspired commission by restaurateur *extraordinaire* Jeremy King, and his wife Debra Hauer, a well-known producer, who had long wanted to build their own house. It was a question of 'first find your architects', as they only started looking for land after becoming firm friends with Jan Kaplicky and Amanda Levete, of the small architectural practice Future Systems. Having written to every estate agent in a six-mile radius around Clerkenwell, King and Hauer finally settled on a small, narrow plot of land that boasted the dubious blessing of three large trees with preservation orders attached. What started off as abstract sketches and strange-shaped models by Future Systems in response to the constraints of the site (including the space occupied by the aforementioned

12

trees) slowly matured into a home in the shape of a transparent, right-angled triangle. This inventive design made the most of the available space, and of the light. Thanks to a moment of clear-sightedness on the part of the local council, planning permission was granted four to one in favour of a 'unique dwelling'. Upon completion, *The Architect's Journal* used the same adjective, as well it could, for this house is completely original in its conception: translucent yet functional, sensuous yet practical, lyrical, and still private. Sandwiched between two solid flanking walls, the rest of the exterior structure is of glass. One enters along a gangplank that skirts a venerable ash tree, into a triple-height entrance hall. Stairs immediately stretch across the width of the house, climbing steeply upwards to the glass roof and the scuttling clouds beyond. On the top floor, the master bedroom seems to be suspended in the sky; on the floor below, the glass wall of the children's playroom and bedroom gives you the impression of being in a treehouse. Both bedrooms have bathroom pods in the ingenious central 'nervous system' situated directly behind the stairs, where wiring, pipes and storage are hidden away. The ground floor consists of a dining room and kitchen, overlooked by a mezzanine lounge, and responding to King and Hauer's desire 'for a non-specific living area'. Throughout there is a sense of space and light, an awareness of beauty allied to modernity that is about as poetic as architecture can get. Other than a 'surprise third baby', whose arrival made the house feel suddenly smaller, 'the toughest problem was insulation — overheating in summer and keeping warm in winter', solved by a complex system of blinds, heating and ventilation. Hauer and King's faith in their architects – 'we were only galvanized into building by a desire to have Future Systems think something up for us' – has been richly rewarded, and all this to the tightest of budgets that would only just have permitted them to buy and restore a 'more normal' family house in the same area. And the additional pleasure of writing a chapter in the history of domestic architecture in London was included in the price.

Debra Hauer & Jeremy King

On the previous pages: a portrait of Jeremy King and Debra Hauer. The detail shows an abseiling window cleaner hard at work on their 'glass house' in Islington, one of the most important architectural achievements for domestic use in London in the 1990s. *Left*: a view of the walkway which curves past the ash tree that boasts a preservation order and thus determined the very shape of the house. Through the thick glass bricks of the relatively discreet street façade one only gets the vaguest idea of the architectural merit of the house. The view from the back garden, *right*, gives a much truer idea of it.

On the previous pages: a view of the ground-floor, multi-purpose playroom/dining room, with chairs by Marcel Breuer grouped around a custom-designed glass dining table. On the wall on the right hangs an important triptych by the Boyle family. The stairs lead to a mezzanine sitting room. *Left*: a view of the aluminum stairs which zigzag behind the glass-brick façade, leading to three upper floors. *Above*: a view of the yellow bathroom pod. All the bathrooms, wiring and storage have been housed in a central pod structure that runs through the height of the house. *Right*: the main bedroom on the top floor, with its tree-top view of the highest branches of the ancient trees in the back garden.

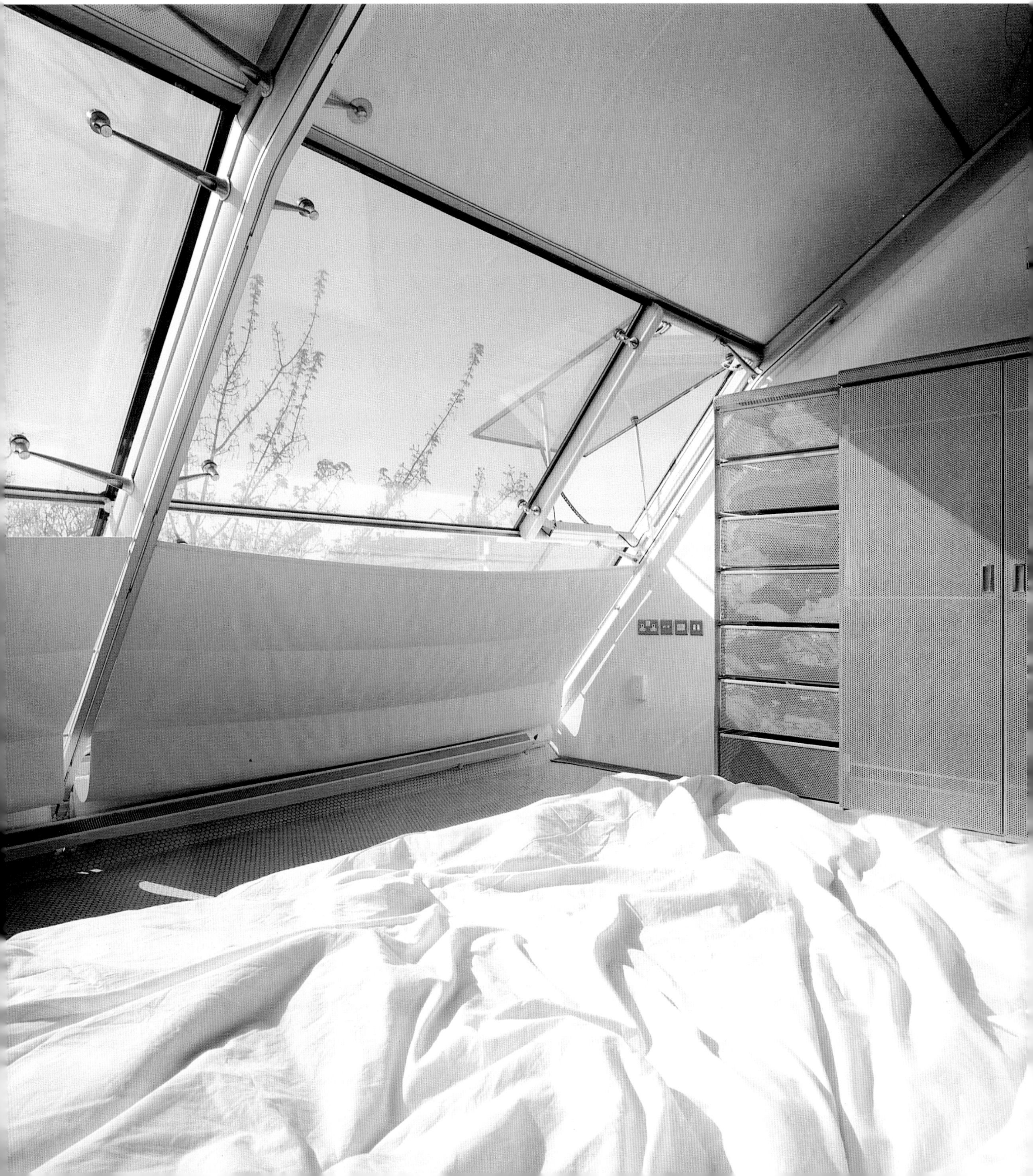

Peter Hinwood's public career began with a brief and unforeseen moment of stardom in the classic cult film, *The Rocky Horror Picture Show*, in which he played the unforgettably beautiful android. He then redirected his artistic inclinations into the less demanding, and more challenging, field of the decorative arts. As an antique dealer, Hinwood 'is involved in the pursuit of creating a harmonious environment by combining a wide range of artefacts from different epochs and cultures, and attempting to pass on the message'. Educated at Stowe, a celebrated public school and the grandest of eighteenth-century houses, he plunged straight into the radically different world of swinging Chelsea in the late 1960s. Greatly inspired by friend and neighbour Christopher Gibbs, he discovered both the art of high bohemia and the funky early 1970s lifestyle. He also made his first trips to Morocco, 'with the Rolling Stones around it was that whole flower-power thing, and such fun. Tangier in particular was like a stage set in dreamland'. There he discovered a culture that continues to fascinate him, and has left its very distinctive mark on his London

13

apartment. 'I go there to unwind and end up bringing back souvenirs of my most relaxed moments, which encourage me to think positively. To be truthful, the most distinguished Moroccan pieces have been found in Great Britain. Variety is all-important; mixing rich and poor things together, treasures with rubbish, so to speak, stimulates the senses.' His large, first-floor flat, which has agreeably noble proportions and wonderfully high ceilings, was built in the eighteenth century, and became the home of the speaker of the House of Commons after the First World War. The Mayfair building was converted into flats in the 1950s, and Hinwood has lived here for almost twenty years. He discovered it when he was called in to look at a painting by the former resident; he bought the painting and immediately asked for first refusal on the flat. 'I liked the idea of living in what was originally a drawing room. There was something about it, with its big windows, that evoked the artist's studio. It was then incredibly

grand, but I thought it would make a good background.' Apart from the mass of textiles, ceramics, oriental bits and pieces and tiles, which evoke the eclectic tastes of such painter collectors as Lord Leighton, the first thing that strikes you about Hinwood's home is the luminous walls. They are green: 'the bright lime wash you sometimes see in Morocco. I didn't want a solid colour, so first I painted the walls with several layers of white for transparency. Then I found an importer of ordinary Turkish house paints, who stocked the bright, cheerful colours and mad mixtures I like. It's a wonderful colour because it ensures that the flat never feels grey and depressing, or too "Londony".' From Hinwood's large, eighteenth-century, painted kitchen table, which doubles as a desk, scattered with illustrious fragments of statuary, one can examine the dull slate roofs of the adjacent mews. London is just across the window sill, and yet in Hinwood's fresh and vibrant interior, it seems many moons away.

Peter Hinwood

On the previous pages: a portrait of Peter Hinwood, and a detail of some favourite tiles. *Left and above*: two views of the main room; an eighteenth-century painted kitchen table with a scrubbed pine top holds an accumulation of favourite objects, including an antique Roman marble head standing on a sixteenth-century Florentine base carved with the head of an angel; a fourteenth-century Egyptian candlestick and hammam bowl; and a pair of eighteenth-century Turkish candlesticks found in Marrakech. *On the following pages*: a large English, Regency, carved sofa upholstered in red velvet is the centre point of the room. It is surrounded by paintings and objects which express Hinwood's eclectic taste.

Opposite: in the bedroom can be seen a pair of English, green-painted kitchen tables with scrubbed tops, *circa* 1840; these were once stolen and later happily recovered; the painting of the dog is Irish and eighteenth century, and above it hangs an African barber's sign in painted wood. *Above*: the iron bed, painted green, is probably French, *circa* 1820, and is covered with an African textile. The eighteenth-century Turkish cupboard is inlaid with tortoiseshell, mother-of-pearl and bone. *Left*: another detail of the bedroom, showing an eighteenth-century leather armchair in elm, and a Victorian English barber's pole.

Opposite: a view of Hinwood's delightfully unpretentious kitchen, painted bright blue and tiled in black and white in a chessboard pattern in order to evoke the humble little butchers' shops of Morocco. *Above*: the bathroom relies for its effect on an ingenious play of reflections in the many mirrors; the small, round ones are concave as opposed to the more usual convex models, and are therefore quite frighteningly deforming! The colour scheme is once again black and white, and framed prints, striped tiles and a graphic African barber's sign add to the unusual atmosphere.

Matthias Sauerbruch and Louisa Hutton are partners, both romantically and at the desks of their bipolar architectural practice, 'where we sit opposite each other all day'. They met as students at the Architectural Association in Bedford Square, and soon plunged themselves into the fascinating sphere of architectural competitions, 'partly for getting jobs, but also for fun'. In 1989, they formed their own practice, living and working in London and Berlin, and becoming quite thoroughly bicultural. Often winning prizes and being subsequently commissioned, they continue to enjoy preparing for competitions. It is a highly stimulating way of working, which inspires a constant reappraisal of architectural enigmas, and perhaps explains the freshness of their projects. 'We have been working so closely for so long that although there might be an initial tendency for me to work more particularly on the colours and the details, and for Matthias to work on the conceptual side of things, over the years our roles have overlapped and merged. Our projects are very much the expression of the two of us, and working on so many competitions has helped that.'

14

Sauerbruch and Hutton are modernists, but with a romantic bloom to their work. After so many years of hard-edged white cubes, and radical minimalism on offer under the label of 'contemporary domestic architecture', it is most refreshing to discover that when they mention the Bauhaus it is to evoke its – often overlooked – teaching of the importance of colour. When Louisa discusses their London home, situated in an apparently unexceptional terraced house close to Portobello market, it is with a clear sense of fun, a sensualist's delight in the materials, and a vivacious appraisal of its visual impact. The 1890s building houses both their London office and their *pied-à-terre*. The complete architectural reworking of the space is not immediately apparent, as the façade has been left untouched in order to respect the planners' demands. As you enter, the lower floors are relatively subdued: functional, modernistic offices decorated in a range of greys, natural wood and a touch of lavender. 'We liked the idea of the house evolving slowly upwards, the colour getting stronger and the spaces becoming more adventurous. Floor by floor, there is less of the Victoriana and more and more of our intervention. The top two floors, where the flat is, are much more intense than the rest.' It is in their private eyrie that the true glory of Sauerbruch and Hutton's sense of space reveals itself. For a start, there is no roof, only clear glass suspended from steel joists so that the changing sky of swirling clouds or bright-blue heaven becomes their splendid ceiling. Then there are no walls, apart from the party walls; there is colour, lots of festive, unexpected, glorious colour. A vibrant, deliciously hot, 'family of reds' contrast with the sky; one bright-yellow surface looks like 'rapeseed in Norfolk in August' against the ceiling of storm clouds. It is not the walls that are so deeply, brightly coloured with pigment suspended in a glaze over an eggshell base, but the couple's 'furniture boxes', used to store all the mess of daily life tidily out of sight. Even the kitchen, part of this skylit room, is invisible apart from a slate surface and a minimalist black tap. In this living-dining-cooking space, the white walls are smooth and powdery with plaster imported from Germany; the oak floorboards are warm, with underfloor heating. Immediately downstairs is another deconstructed space, part-library, part-bathroom and bedroom; folding doors and a fold-out bed mean that a guest bedroom can be created in a few minutes. One 'box' in indigo is entirely used to house books, while perpendicular volumes in magenta and yew-veneer provide storage and form the necessary divisions for this more intimate sleeping-reading-bathing space. Such attention to detail makes Sauerbruch and Hutton's home an inspired project, a reference for a new kind of colourful modern minimalism.

Louisa Hutton &
Matthias Sauerbruch

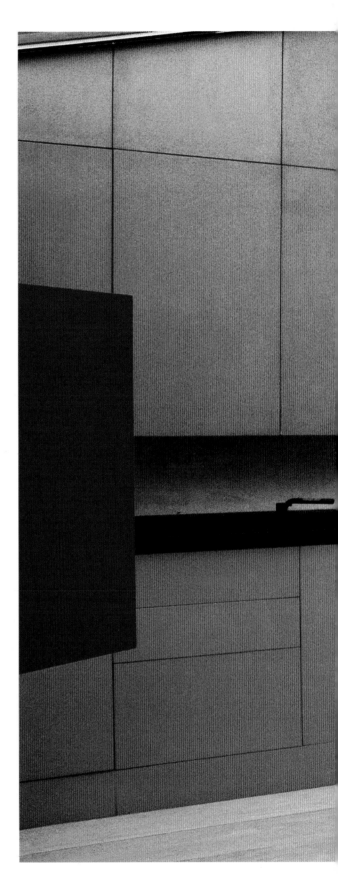

On the preious pages: a portrait of Louisa Hutton and Matthias Sauerbruch, and a night view of the house from above. *Above*: a detail of the top-floor living space, showing the dining table designed by the architects, and chairs picked up at a junk shop. The 'furniture box' on the wall is a bookcase, and the lamp on the left is by Schliephacke. *Right*: another view of the same room, showing the 'invisible' kitchen; the slate surface incorporates black sinks and a flat, black hob. Behind, the kitchen cupboards become a plane of pure, bright colour, and take on a decorative aspect which is enhanced by the contrast with the equally bright tones of other storage 'boxes'.

Left: a view of the seating area on the top floor. The canvas awnings that are used to shade the room from the summer sun that pours through the glass roof add a softer edge to the room, as well as performing their essential function. *Below*: on the second floor, the palette is quite different; the bathroom, bedroom and library are smaller and more intimate spaces, and yew veneer has also been used, as well as blocks of solid colour. *Bottom*: in the bathroom, the 'bruised' colour of the door was achieved with an indigo glaze over a salmon base, and 'boxes' in a series of greens are set into the white plastic wall to provide storage space.

Emma Kennedy is a true hippy chick. She is the kind of well-brought-up, but fiercely independent, 'London girl' that fashion designers coo over at castings. They know full well that this kind of girl will give a particularly edgy allure to their creations. From Twiggy through to Kate Moss, England has a tradition of producing these tall, leggy creatures exhibiting coltish grace, and with their heads screwed on the right way. Kennedy was a model for six years, spending most of her career in Japan, 'just because I enjoyed being there so much. Japan was an amazing experience'. Striking-looking, and obviously clever, since winning a loan from the Prince's Youth Business Trust in 1992 together with her partner Monique Low, Kennedy has set up a company and opened a shop. She has designed and produced 'hundreds and hundreds' of hand-painted or sandblasted glasses under the suitably upbeat label, Funky Stuff. The stuff is indeed funky: irregularly shaped glasses on crooked stems boast painted stars, suns, fruit or flowers straight out of some excessive psychedelic cartoon. Three years into their business the two associates realized that

15

'the majority of time was spent on running a shop and not on painting'. Together they hit upon the idea of working out of a studio and 'receiving visitors and commissions' from Tuesday to Saturday. Kennedy thus feels herself a decorative artist once more, and not just a shopkeeper. Her home, as one would expect, also reflects the 'peace and love' aesthetic that is present in her painting work and wardrobe alike. It is a bohemian pad, reflecting her extensive travels as a model, but also her professional interest in decoration. The result is a fresh take on the London interior, an invigorating environment in gold leaf and candy-wrapper colours. The bottom-floor flat in a Fulham house, it benefited greatly from the kaleidoscopic vision of bright, saturated colours that Kennedy had brought back from a trip to Mexico. 'I originally wanted to paint the walls orange and blue, but I did tons of colour trials and the red was amazing … ' 'About that time I had a friend who worked at the salvage yard L.A.S.S. CO., and I used to spend Saturdays mooning around there, fascinated. There were lots of bits and pieces out of the Savoy, which was being refurbished. I fell in love with a pair of tatty but outrageous gold curtains that nobody else wanted … I ended up decorating the living room around them. In fact, the whole house was conceived around things rescued from the salvage yard.' As a marked contrast to the red and gold, Kennedy's bedroom is a perfectly simple sanctuary, in which even the floorboards are painted white. 'I don't know why — it is a bit of a contrast — but it just seemed to be right to have a bedroom that was unbelievably romantic.' The bathroom leads off it, so that, in a house that is always full of friends, Kennedy has her own, 'very private' quarters. While the living room evokes an opium-eater's den, and the bedroom is dreamy, the kitchen is 'pure pop'. As for the garden, it is more Copacabana than Fulham, and boasts a bar with a twinkling neon sign that says 'Château le funk'. Of course.

Emma Kennedy

On the previous pages: a portrait of Emma Kennedy and a detail of the garden at her Fulham home, in which she has installed a bright-blue neon sign with the logo from her old glassware shop, 'Château le funk'. *Left and below*: a view of the living room on the ground floor, whose upbeat palette was inspired by a trip to Mexico. Liberal applications of gold leaf add to the exotic atmosphere. The glasses on the table are of her own design.

On these pages: several views of the unusually designed kitchen, conceived by Kennedy herself; the areas for cooking and eating merge, thereby creating a flexible, modern space. It has the added advantage of a conservatory-style skylight, and has been adapted to her informal lifestyle and her love of the colours and cultures of distant lands. Rather than being specifically Mexican in conception, it evokes a wider range of influences, including pop art. The detail, *above right*, shows kitchen utensils from the Mediterranean, Morocco and Asia.

The romantic bedroom, *opposite*, with its en-suite bathroom, *below*, creates a free-flowing space with a loft-like atmosphere seldom found in English terraced houses. The white-painted floorboards add to this impression. Kennedy built the dividing wall reluctantly, as a concession to the need for privacy in the bathroom. Her original idea was to have her antique bath on feet standing in the bedroom. The antique wooden bed is French, and was bought at L. A. S. S. CO., as was much of the furniture in the house, including the oversized mirror propped up against the wall.

The most eclectic of today's great fashion photographers, Nick Knight is on the cutting edge of fashion, his vision finely honed, his multiple references carefully researched, and his visual universe exploding with a myriad of new and innovative techniques. Thus it does not come as a surprise that in the row of identical, gabled suburban homes, his should be the white cube that raised eyebrows and caused petitions to be signed. Built on the plot of land on which Knight's parents had originally built their own, 'very 1956, very Festival of Britain' home, the half-built new house was dubbed a 'Knightmare' by the local community. While unimaginative neighbours clamoured for the house to be bulldozed, the conciliatory Knights adapted their front elevation, and began a close collaboration with architect David Chipperfield. 'Meeting David was decisive. We knew that we wanted something forward-looking, clean and relatively futuristic. We decided very sensibly to interview three architects and then take our decision; we did not want to be caught out. However, as soon as we met David — that was it!' Building their own house was something of a

16

family tradition, as Knight's parents had themselves built several family homes with different architects. 'As a child, the only time that I did not live in a new house was when my father was posted to Paris. I remember being a very bewildered six-year-old in a classical nineteenth-century apartment at Porte Dauphine. It was probably lovely, but it felt most odd at the time …' The initial discussions with Chipperfield were fairly abstract, evoking interconnecting spaces, a central tower-like structure, and different ways of using the rooms … Charlotte Knight remembers: 'At the time Nick was working fairly intensively for Yohji Yamamoto, and I remember thinking that David's attitude to architecture was somewhat similar to Yohji's attitude to clothes – it was all about the essence of things.' The house took eleven months to complete, and came in roughly to budget: 'If it did cost slightly more than we had first envisaged, it was because we ended up deciding not to compromise on the raw materials.' The Knights then set about furnishing their new home with classic design pieces by Alvar Aalto and Marcel Breuer. 'The light is so beautiful that you don't really need much furniture or pictures on the walls.' Their garden, ethereal and Japanese in inspiration, slowly grew to maturity. Silver birches and flowering trees reflected themselves peacefully in the pond, lined with big, green pebbles and edged with black grasses. Then came the bombshell: the 'pink fairies', Emily and Ella May, were born with only a year and a half between them. The house suddenly had to be urgently rethought. 'Although Charlotte and I had been together for years, we just hadn't thought about the possibility of children when we built the house', admits Knight. 'There were holes designed into the floor as light wells, no banisters, narrow stairways, and all kind of fittings that weren't remotely childproof — worst of all, there was no children's room …' All kinds of adaptations were quickly made, and Knight's glorious studio on the first floor was transformed into a stunning children's bedroom, complete with a toy wigwam and an extensive dressing-up wardrobe. Since then, the children have also managed to impose brightly coloured finger paintings on the previously bare walls. A couple of years later, however, 'the house suddenly seemed curiously small, and we started to look longingly at the 1950s monstrosity next door'. The neighbours, of course, had visions of Knight using the house next door as a studio, and raised their voices in protest once again. They were wrong — it is domestic space that the Knights need, and indeed it is to become a Chipperfield-designed extension. In the meantime, the 'pink fairies' fantasize about its gabled, post-Victorian charms: 'to the kids, "a proper house" looks a lot more exciting than minimalism', confesses Knight with a grin.

Charlotte & Nick Knight

On the previous pages: a portrait of the Knights' daughters, Emily and Ella May, dressed as fairies in pink. The detail shows the exterior of the low-slung, David Chipperfield-designed house in Petersham. *Opposite*: the first-floor studio space which Knight has only ever really used to photograph still lifes, and which has now become a children's playroom. The chair, right, in cast iron, is one of the first editions of André Dubreuil's Spine chair. *Above*: a view of the minimalist living room, with a view of the budding, Japanese-inspired garden. The chairs in the foreground are by Marcel Breuer.

Opposite: a view of the elongated dining table designed by Chipperfield, and stools by Marcel Breuer. Like all the furniture in the house, these are simple pieces that have reduced their decorative expression to the essence of their function. The stairs in the background, which lead to the first floor, illustrate a related statement of architectural purity. *Above*: a view from the dining-room table across the hall, and into the living room.

The collaborative works of artists Ben Langlands and Nikki Bell are essentially concerned with the nature of architecture, and how built environments at once reflect and determine human behaviour, so discovering their home seems particularly significant. The couple aim at exploring the interrelationship between people, furniture and buildings, and the fact of living where they do has in itself influenced their work. Their home, built in 1790, is hidden away down a street with a Dickensian name, in the wastes of Whitechapel, in London's East End. Amid the council blocks and post-war architectural horrors, a handful of Georgian terraces have survived with their simple dignity almost intact. In one of these small, four-storey houses, Langlands and Bell have created a spotlessly white world of their own. Close by looms the new mosque, with its gold dome, for the Bengalis and Pakistanis are the latest in the successive waves of immigrants to have made this corner of the East End their own. In sweatshops and on home sewing machines they continue their Jewish predecessors' involvement in the rag trade. Shops selling sweetmeats

17

in impossibly fluorescent colours, with names like 'chum chum' or 'gulab jamin', rub shoulders with local landmarks like the building that housed the freak show in which John Merrick, 'The Elephant Man', was discovered, or the Royal Hospital in which he died. The neighbouring tenement block in which the artists previously lived has sprouted fluttering saris in saturated colours at every window. The pub at the end of the street, previously owned by George the Pole (a refugee Polish count) and his wife, Countess Eileen – East End notables who knew the infamous Kray brothers as babies – is now a 'very good' Pakistani restaurant. 'We have witnessed a gradual transformation', Nikki Bell remarks while serving white coffee in black mugs in her black-and-white basement kitchen, 'when we first moved here there were still lots of Jewish shops and restaurants, often with synagogues at the back. The Bengalis have now taken over in much the same way that the Jews did from the Welsh and Irish before them. The area has always attracted waves of immigrants — it's cheap and near the docks.' Langlands and Bell are passionately knowledgeable about local lore: 'There is real life all around us, and a feeling of the layered history of the place.' Their home was probably speculatively built during the lead-up to the Napoleonic Wars following floor plans in a pattern book. It was not a boom period, and the houses were probably not meant to last much more than sixty years. They were relatively humble homes, and at some point must have housed two families per floor. The occasional neo-classical detailing reinforces the impression of the essential simplicity of the architecture. The houses have one panelled-wood partition running the entire height of the rooms, and the other internal walls are in brick, unlike the earlier and grander Georgian houses, in which wood panelling was the only internal division. Langlands and Bell bought the house at auction, despite advice to the contrary from friends, who told them that they were 'completely mad'. Not bidding until the last moment, they were 'in shock' at finding themselves home-owners. 'The house was in very bad condition, and had no kitchen or bathrooms. It took about a year of hard work —fourteen hours a day and seven days a week — to make it habitable. We did everything ourselves.' They knocked down all the walls, so that each floor became one large, less structured space. The concept of 'decoration' has been pared down to two elements: white and wood. A thick, and sometimes shiny, white paint on the floorboards and walls has reduced the space to 'just a brick box' that allows the fascinating character of the building to shine through. The house is thick with the atmosphere of the past. Langlands and Bell have succeeded in creating a home with all the aesthetic and intellectual characteristics of their art.

Ben Langlands
&Nikki Bell

On the previous pages: a portrait of Ben Langlands and Nikki Bell, and a detail of their living room. Little furniture interferes with the space; the two hand-made, rustic stools were found in the street, and are probably eighteenth century. *Opposite*: a view of the bathroom in their workshop, designed by Ashley Hicks, one of Langlands and Bell's close friends, with whom they previously shared the workshop building. *Right*: the artwork *Traces of Living*, and an elongated table that contains an imaginary museum of the East End, past and present. Many of the objects under glass were found during the restoration of the house. All the clutter of everday life is stowed neatly away in tall, simple cupboards.

In deepest Bermondsey, behind a soup kitchen and the delightful surprise of an impossibly picturesque pub, lies 'The Glasshouse', in which Andrew Logan dreams up his flamboyant sculptures in mirror, resin and glass. The house, designed by architect and urban visionary Michael Davis, corresponds perfectly to Logan's work. Davis is deeply influenced by the bright planes of colour favoured by Mexican architect Luis Barragán. These colours – hot pinks, deep sea greens and tender orange – are characteristic of Logan's art. Entering at ground level through a large turquoise room that combines the functions of kitchen, dining room and a corridor-like office, the true genius of the architect's work does not become apparent until one ascends into the enormous, first-floor studio. There Davis has created a unique space, in which a triangular glass roof dwarfs what appears to be a small, brightly coloured Spanish house, complete with red geraniums in its window boxes, and violet bougainvillea climbing up the façade. The effect is surreal. This independent structure houses the bedrooms and bathrooms; the rest of the floor space is given over

to Logan's giant sculptures. Past the studio lies the patio garden, from which the whole effect can be admired. The couple had previously lived in another unusual transparent structure, on the roof of a building near Liverpool Street station. It was thought to be an early 1920s film studio, built in glass to satisfy the pioneering film-makers' technical demands for natural light. Logan and Davis were dislodged in 1988, when that area of the City was considerably redeveloped. The present 'glasshouse' was previously a garage and workshop. 'I have always had studios with fantastic views, and then someone would come along and build an atrocity right in front of it … so this time we decided on a glass roof. No one can spoil a view of the universe!' Logan, whose work was defined by critic Jasia Reichardt as being 'the art of popular poetry and metropolitan glamour', is a craftsman of excess, a sculptor of fantasy, and a cheerfully decadent *bon vivant*. He first shot into the news in the early 1970s as the 'host and hostess' — half man, half woman — presenter of the 'Alternative Miss World' competition, a rollicking art event, and a spoof on the beauty pageant. Ever since, he has been a giant figure in the fringe of the transatlantic showbiz underworld, as a initiator of many high moments of camp. Derek Jarman once made a film called *Andrew Logan kissing 25 personalities*, and even now, twenty-five years later, Logan continues to combine theatrical events with his work in sculpture and jewellery. Speaking of the latter, which is mirror encrusted and multi-coloured, George Melly, with his characteristic enthusiasm called Logan a contemporary Fabergé. On the opening of his Museum of Sculpture in Wales, *The Independent* rather acutely classified him as 'the Wizard of Odd'. All of Logan's accessible extravaganza, such as the giant flowers that were a feature of Biba's famous roof garden, the monumental Pegasus, and the balancing butterflies, work perfectly with Davis's interior. The colour, he says, 'was because of the light — with a glass roof you have to avoid white, or you would be practically blinded … so I took the colours of Rajasthan and Mexico, and painted downstairs like a blue swimming pool'. The deep, saturated colours of the walls, 'painted with the same paint that Ludwig of Bavaria used for his pink palaces, because it sinks into the plaster and makes the colours more vibrant', contrast with the gilded supporting beams and the resin flooring in saffron. The atmosphere is dynamic, even on the greyest day. 'It has become so wonderful here that I hardly go out', muses Logan, while sipping lemonade made from fresh lemons that grow effortlessly in the 'greenhouse effect'. The artist long ago attained cult status, and his home richly deserves it too — it is as colourful and unpredictable as he is.

Andrew Logan &
Michael Davis

On the previous pages: a portrait of Michael Davis, and the façade of his distinctive home and studio in Bermondsey, known as 'The Glasshouse'. Architect Michael Davis was greatly inspired by the palette of Mexican architect Luis Barragán, and his method of using powdery, distempered washes of different tones of virbrancy and intensity. *Opposite*: 'Pegasus', with his mirrored wings, is well over man-sized, but the glass-roofed studio is large enough to accommodate him and friends, *below*.

Opposite, above and below: the bedroom, with a collection of portraits and photographs of friends hung on the curved wall behind the bed, which is itself covered with a brightly striped counterpane. *Above*: a view of the dining table in the open-plan kitchen-cum-library, the first room encountered upon entering. It's a happy jumble that scarcely prepares the visitor for the grandeur of the immense, skylit studio above.

Celia Lyttelton is bubbly, funny, enormously talented, and completely unpredictable. She paints, etches, writes and dabbles in television. She has been the driving force behind a significant art gallery, and is filmed giving surrealist dinner parties. She has posed for some painters and has backed others, members of her group of multi-cultural friends. She travels passionately, for months at a time, in the Yemen. She is famous for her stylishly outlandish outfits: her wardrobe is as original as she is, revealing an undisciplined clutter of priceless antiques and contemporary couture. Recently, however, she has been upstaged, in the nicest possible way, by her husband, Andrew Heath. A mathematics don, often rather retiring, he surprised everyone in their circle by suddenly announcing that he wanted to become an actor. Acting classes came next, then auditions and the first successes — Heath seems poised on the edge of a fully fledged artistic career. In short, this is no ordinary couple, and their home poetically expresses their individuality. When discovered for the first time, it seems a romantic daydream of an urban retreat. 'I wanted the effect of

19

mildew coming through the walls, like in old palaces in India' – Lyttelton is studying the mottled violet, butter and pistachio of the first-floor drawing-room walls as she speaks. The treatment which she has given the walls throughout the house ranges from Renaissance fresco techniques involving gesso and real rabbit-skin glue in the dining room, to beeswax on the plaster in the stairwell. Throughout, a beautiful luminosity is preserved, giving the walls a living quality which Lyttelton calls 'a soft-centred Mark Rothko effect', and is part of the legacy of growing up 'surrounded by frescoes' in Italy. In the drawing room, the palette was influenced by the deep blue and brilliant yellow of a painting of a canary by Craigie Aitchison that the artist gave her. 'I'd been posing for him, and he had been plying me with vodka and tonic and egg sandwiches, and then he asked me to choose, which was so nice of him. The frame was made by Ewan Uglow, which is a funny coincidence as they were at the Slade together.' Lyttelton has also posed for Uglow who, by all reports, was a harder man to please, and got quite furious when she came back a shade browner from holiday. Lyttelton and Heath have designated one floor of the house for separate activities; this floor qualifies itself for pleasure, 'there is a spare bed and a bean sack on the floor, so that despite the rather grand sofa it does not feel too formally decadent'. In the converted attic, which lies under the white-painted eaves and joists that have been revealed by removing the ceiling, lies the book-lined study. It is here that Celia works at her books and articles, and does some of her drawing, although a lot of her more painterly work is done at the remote cottage in Yorkshire that is their most private refuge. The ground floor is where Lyttelton stages her renowned surrealist suppers, at which guests might eat any of the peculiar concoctions beloved of the Italian Futurist Marinetti, who abhorred pasta and never tired of proposing rather more exciting combinations of food to his countrymen. On an 'ordinary' night, Heath might prepare an impromptu macrobiotic picnic in the wilds of the prettily overgrown garden; if not, guests will eat in the dining room that leads off the kitchen, in which some of designer Jasper Morrison's prized first pieces give a contemporary twist. The ceiling has been left decorated with swirls of soot, the legacy of a fire. The walls have an unexpected sheen that glows in the candlelight. 'This room, somehow, makes people never want to leave: they come for lunch and leave at 3 am … but then this house is a complete escape; it's about comfort and my whole ethos of how I want to live. It has a little of all the houses I've ever loved … but enough for me to go on hundreds of imaginary journeys without ever leaving the front door.'

Celia Lyttelton & Andrew Heath

On the previous pages: a portrait of Celia Lyttelton, and a detail of her garden at her Notting Hill home. *Opposite*: the dining room. The table and chairs are very early pieces by Jasper Morrison. *Below*: a view of the first-floor reception room. The sofa, upholstered in 'Aitchison blue', sits theatrically by the boldly striped blue-and-yellow canvas curtains, painted by Lyttelton with Liquidex and the aid of masking tape (to get the stripes straight).

Left: another view of the 'L-shaped' reception room on the first floor, showing the guest bed in the corner. It is festooned with fabric from Indonesia and also from Lyttelton's friend, Celia Birtwell. The curtain is painted with 'what everyone always thinks is a dartboard, but was in fact inspired by a visit to an exhibition on Buddhism'. The walls, glazed and rubbed down with a very personal recipe involving gesso and rabbit-skin glue in the manner of the Renaissance painters, are a particularly intangible combination of violet, green, yellow and the most subtle of pinks.

Above: a view of the library. 'It is meant to evoke a ship, with the stripped wood floor and the white rafters; each time we come up here we like to think that we are about to leave on a new "journey of the mind".' It is a pleasant room: large, airy, and somehow far removed from the bustle of Ladbroke Grove below, featuring, right, a chair in cast iron by André Dubreuil.
Right: another view of the library, showing the distressed white shelving well loaded with books; the floorboards were painted with specially mixed colours. The portrait of Lyttelton is by Paul Benny.

That Tiggy Maconochie met her American husband in Tangier seems curiously appropriate for this high-flying photographer's agent, who has always maintained that 'I *never* think of myself as English…'. Looking after such significant photographers as Helmut Newton, Jeanloup Sieff or Horst, her work often takes her travelling, and she is never happier than when traipsing around far-flung corners of the world, her own camera in hand, and accompanied by her book-loving husband. Budnik is a film art director who collects rare books, and is 'capable of digging out a first edition from the dusty shelves of second-hand shops from Streatham to Santa Fe'. They share an unusual space, created out of the ground floor of a conventional Victorian terraced house. Maconochie calls it 'friendly minimal', and it is an inspiring take on the art of one-room living. 'Initially, it had been gutted and converted into a dance studio, and later into a recording room for one of Peter Gabriel's musicians. Although it was only one oddly shaped room, I knew I wanted to live there as soon as I saw it; it had enormous potential: lots of light, space and a tiny walled garden.'

20

Despite the estate agent's attempt to have her gazumped, the departing musician stood up for her, and Maconochie was able to buy it. With the energy and intensity that characterizes everything she does, she then set about creating her ideal London quarters. Despite having several high-profile architect friends who could have helped her with the project, she chose to 'co-operate' with two young architects, in order to be able to be 'uncompromising' about what she wanted. 'They were great. We had one meeting here squatting on the floor, and they understood all the essential points immediately. The space had to speak for itself, the light had to continue to flow the length of the flat. I wanted only industrial materials to be used, and the splendid wooden floor we had discovered under the lino defined the mood.' In architectural terms, the solution turned out to be a large 'box' within the huge room. This box, in multi-fibre density board cut to show the grain, contains three walk-in cupboards, a large storage space, and two cabin-like bedrooms complete with portholes. One is perched above the main space, with its own ladder and gangplank, from which the photograph on the next pages was taken. The marble chimney breast came from Liverpool Street station's ladies' waiting room, and the screen print above it is by photographer Michael Roberts, whom Maconochie also represents. A nautical feel was again evoked with aluminium and industrial fittings for the 'galley' kitchen. It is, of course, stocked with every imaginable exotic condiment, from Chinese herbs to Mexican peppers. It is separated from the main space by tall, sliding doors, and leads out onto the 'all-white' garden, with its mosaic in mirror and tile by artist Martin Cohen. On summer evenings, it is a simple matter for the couple to drag out their colourful Moroccan cushions, and to 'pretend they are somewhere else'.

Tiggy Maconochie & Aaron Budnik

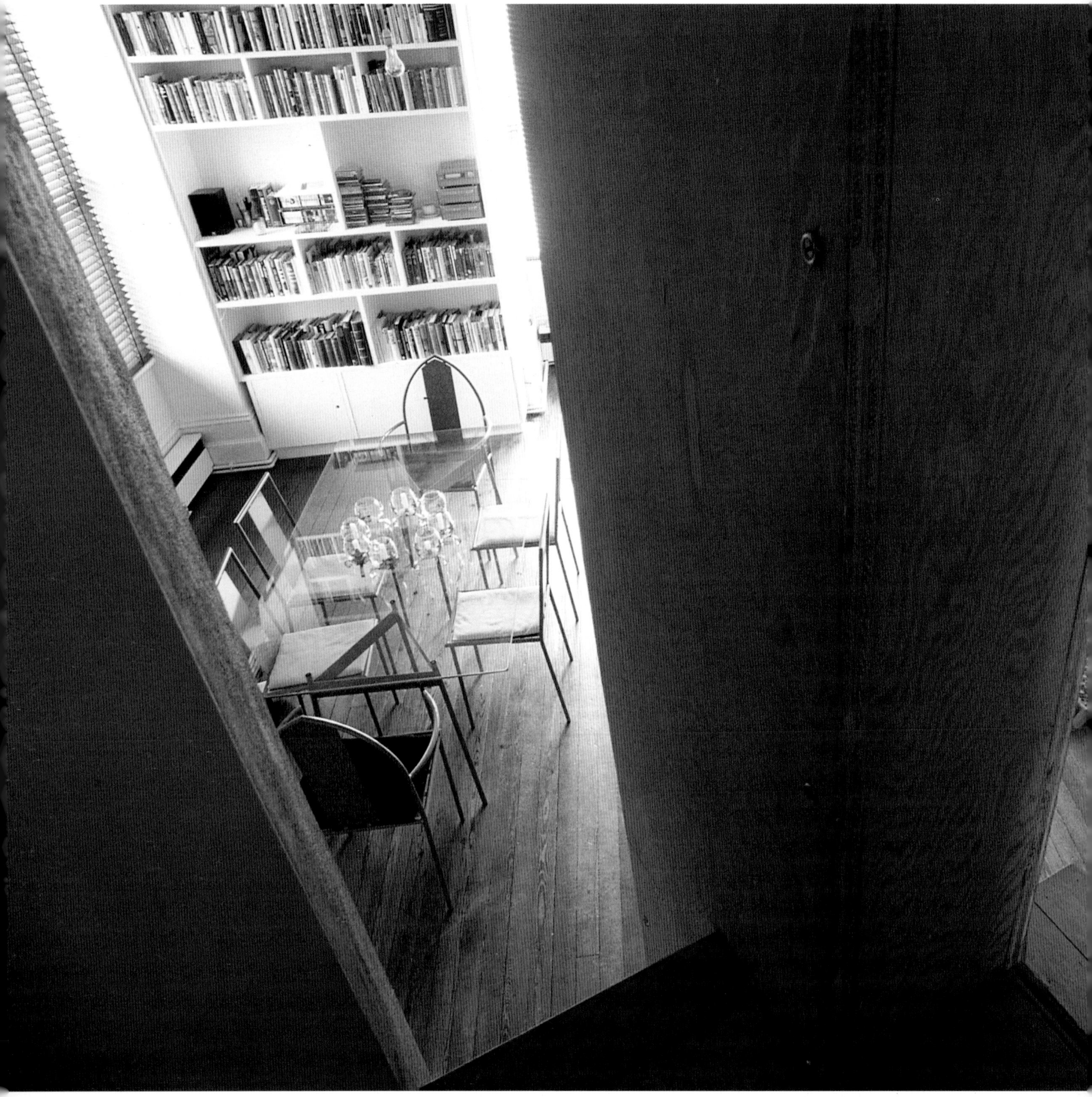

On the previous pages: a portrait of Maconochie and Budnik in their loft-like space, formerly a dance studio, in Clapham. The sliding doors are an ingenious device with which to separate the kitchen from the main living area. The detail shows their back garden and part of a large mosaic on a Moroccan theme by English artist Martin Cohen. *Opposite and above*: the main space, seen from the cabin-like guest bedroom that occupies the top part of the wooden structure, containing storage space and the master bedroom below. The screen print over the fireplace is by Michael Roberts; the embroidered cushions are souvenirs from travels in Morocco.

King's Cross station lies at the tangled nerve centre of London's urban sprawl, and living there would seem to most of us something akin to an inner-city nightmare. However, through one of those contradictions that make the city so engaging, hidden away in the lee of the station is a tranquil pocket of practically untouched late-Georgian buildings. One of these is the particularly interesting, and altogether unexpected abode of Christoph Martin, a young German fashion photographer. He discovered it when, still under the influence of two years of living in New York, he was scouting for London loft spaces. A friend had tipped him off to the fact that British Rail often rented out warehouses quite cheaply. Between St Pancras and King's Cross, he became intrigued by a vast building with boarded-up windows that looked abandoned. When, after numerous enquiries, he at last ascertained to which sub-section of which department he should apply, British Rail agreed to rent it out for a tiny fee, on the condition that a fireproof ceiling was installed. That called for an altogether different type of investment, but Martin was charmed by the

21

building's dilapidated glamour, so he procured himself a flatmate and set to work. The building had been a boxing club, and was littered with the intriguing remnants of its last fight, 'there were cups on the tables, and boxing gloves on the floor — just as if everybody had walked out fully expecting to come back the next day'. Fascinated, Martin decided to keep the 'sporting-club' atmosphere of the place. There were more intriguing revelations to come: the neighbours and old boxing pros who popped around to visit explained the origins of the building, which were much more grandiose than Martin could ever have guessed. It had been known as the *Turnhalle*, or German gymnastic society, and had been designed by Edward Grüning and built in 1864–5. A high-roofed sporting club for expatriate Germans, with a striking first-floor gallery and roof trusses of laminated timber, it was considered prestigious enough to host the boxing events of the first Olympics of the century. It had subsequently been divided up, probably in the 1930s, and Martin's segment represented about a third of the original area. Upstairs, there is a dance studio, and adjacent to Martin's 'loft', a couple of warehouses have been carved out. 'The first thing we did was to fill up a few skips of old rubbish, paint the walls all white, and then experiment on painting the Georgian columns. Like the beams, these were in German steel — the builders had brought all their materials with them in true Teutonic fashion. We finally settled on a bronze colour for them in the main space, and white for the bathroom.' The bathroom, with the sportsmen's row of ancient metal showers still in place, is the most surprising feature of this completely unexpected apartment. It has a strangely Mediterranean atmosphere, as Martin has set up a beach chair, and chose a luminous green for the walls. The main room is big enough to cause a table-tennis table (bought second-hand for £2), a punchball, two large desks and a Chesterfield from a street market all to look slightly lost in the immensity of it all. If the photographic studio lights betray Martin's present profession, the sporty feel is due not only to the building's past, but also to the fact that he used to be a professional sailor, and is still a keen sportsman. He is passionate about his home, and even though the 'decorating' has been done on a shoestring, it certainly reflects the athletic character of the original structure. The splendid old building seems to have fallen into the right hands.

Christoph Martin

On the previous pages: a portrait of Christoph Martin, his cat, and a detail of the dining alcove in his home that is very close to King's Cross station. As was most of the furniture in this former gymnasium, the table was bought for very little in a London market. *Above*: the sofa remains isolated in the centre of the huge space. Martin has included many sport-related items, such as the basketball hoop and a table-tennis table, as a reference to the building's past. *Left*: the bedroom, in a small room separated from the main area, was painted a rusty red directly onto the brickwork. *Opposite*: the impressive bathroom, with its communal showers, which has been left much as it was originally.

'When I first moved onto the boat, I was terrified of feeling permanently seasick. Then I got so used to the rocking that it made me feel quite at home. But I always studied the tide tables: they were absolutely crucial when planning dinner parties. Some friends used to refuse to come at high tide.' When Juliette Mole, actress and decorator, Oxford graduate in Arabic and Turkish, and linguist *extraordinaire,* moved into a houseboat moored by Battersea Bridge, she had never been aboard one before. She was worried about it being hugely impractical, but she needed somewhere to live, urgently. Her mother had seen it in *The Times,* advertised at only £30,000, 'which was all I had and was likely to have. As an actress I could forget about a mortgage. The choice was between a small, dark basement in the outer reaches, or this. I chose this'. Once she moved in, she set to decorating it with the gusto of the born decorator and bargain hunter. 'I had an absolutely wonderful time, the advantage being that because it was so small you could invest in extravagant materials because you needed so little of them. Because of my travels in the Middle East, I had

22

quite a stock of rich textiles and objects, so I intentionally made the interior quite exotic. I desperately wanted to avoid the "twee boating look" of nautical blue and white.' The bedroom was covered in silver paper, with 5,000 upholstery tacks strategically placed 'so that it looked like the inside of a submarine. This was only possible because the bedroom was literally as big as the bed. For the canopied ceiling I only bought a metre of a Timney Fowler fabric, which I edged with shot silk'. The bathroom was done up in gold, and the kitchen 'to everyone's horror', painted black. Mole's training in *trompe l'œil* at Brussels' Ecole Supérieur de Peinture allowed her to add a neoclassical mural to the main cabin: 'I used to recline on a day bed and imagine I was gliding down the Bosphorus ...'. Nautical life only got the better of her once, when, during the infamous storms of 1991, she had to move out for a night as bottles crashed around her and the books jumped out of the bookshelves. 'Then I hit on the idea of secur-

ing them with black knicker elastic, and that didn't happen again.' River living was 'rather like owning a detached house with a Chelsea address, but much more community-minded, as lots of very amusing people live on those boats'. She even had her own garden, the forty-six-foot (fourteen-metre) roof terrace which was her 'pride and joy'. She met her husband, Lloyd Owen, across her gangplank, was married on the boat, and 'broke her heart' by leaving it when she discovered she was pregnant. 'I refused to move any further than just across the bridge, and I still miss my houseboat. I can't go past the boats without wishing we had never left.'

Juliette Mole & Lloyd Owen

On the previous pages: a portrait of the Juliette Mole, and a detail of the main living area in her houseboat moored at Chelsea Wharf. The careful detailing on the curtains, wall finishes and upholstery achieves the impression of being in a real house – Mole was determined to avoid any nautical references. *Above*: the luxurious bedroom cabin, with its silver walls and rich colours. *Opposite, above and below*: another bedroom, and the 'proper' bathroom, with its full-length bath. The accumulation of prints and paintings evoke the kind of drawing-room atmosphere with which houseboat-living is not usually associated.

Andrew Mortada strikes one as being deeply reserved, even timid. He lives hidden away in his east London workshop, and on his own admission 'very rarely leaves it'. This is perhaps one of the reasons why he spent years getting the flat above the workshop exactly right; it is a poetic space, full of planes of colour and beautiful, contrasting textures. Mortada is so self-effacing that it seems rather improbable that he has, in fact, modelled extensively for his neighbour Ricardo Cinalli, and is the inspiration for many of the artist's neo-classical torsos. It is almost as hard to believe that Mortada was a developer during the 1980s 'yuppie' boom period; he seems so much an artisan. He has turned to furniture-making of the earthy, hands-on variety, and produces one-off, or very limited, editions of unusual pieces, 'inspired by 1950s design, the Arts-and-Crafts movement, or tribal art …' Their strong shapes betray his training as a sculptor. The house itself is as introspective as its owner, centred around the well of light over the dining room that evokes an Islamic courtyard, with the living quarters spiralling around it. His home was conceived as 'a series of

23

spaces that would serve different purposes, that would connect and lead into each other'. Inspired by the Villa Roche, a house that Le Corbusier designed for an art collector in the 1930s, Mortada did all the work himself, 'differentiating between the public and private spaces architecturally'. This involved creating a suspended metal walkway, and a geometric mezzanine to overhang the main space. He wanted to divide up the main 'brick rectangle' of each of the four storeys into smaller spaces, to create a feeling of anticipation, of discovery. His modernist additions seem to stand as sculptural installations within the skeleton of the original frame. Mortada was building an expression of himself, to satisfy his 'sense of pride' with regard to how he chose to live. Indeed, the whole project is finished to a highly professional standard, a polished world above the dust and grit of the studio. The organic forms of the 1950s are present in the curved walls, in the smooth, coloured plaster surfaces, and in the aerodynamic light fittings. The sandblasted brick walls contrast with the grainy woods of the ethnic art that he collects, as do the juxtaposition of work space and living space, and the use of both industrial and domestic materials. These stimulating stylistic contradictions closely reflect the enigma of the man himself: the artist's eye contrasts with the workman's hands and build; the love of colour and sensuous forms diverge from the roughness implied in stripping the walls of his home down to their structural London brick.

Andrew Mortada

On the previous pages: Andrew Mortada in his kitchen, and a detail of the double-height space that he has designed over his dining room. The attention-grabbing lighting fixture was designed by Mortada from a series of paper lanterns. *Above*: an ethnic pot against the simple lines of the chimney breast. *Opposite*: the same room is seen from ground level; the oval wooden table of Mortada's design echoes the sensuous shape of the lanterns and the African sculptures that he collects. The smoothly plastered gallery balustrade contrasts with the raw brick of the walls.

Above: the well-equipped kitchen, and *right*, the Japanese-inspired tub in the bathroom on the top floor. *Opposite*: the bedroom, with its sloping ceiling. A suspended walkway connects it to the bathroom.

From his Fitzrovia studio, painter and illustrator Lawrence Mynott has a charming stroll through some of Bloomsbury's most elegant squares to his home. With his jaunty moustache and his velour fedora, he cuts a dashing figure. Accompanied, as he often is, by his chinese-crested dog, he looks like nothing so much as one of his own illustrations. The home he has decorated with his graphic-designer wife Anthea, is just as surprising. From the outside, it looks strangely like a Japanese restaurant. 'We once got a group of lost Japanese knocking at the front door and asking to see the menu …', Lawrence recalls, laughing. This impression is created by the rather smart, made-to-measure wooden blinds that shield the ground-floor flat, 'with its own front door', from the street. Once inside the Edwardian building, however, the references are rather more Orientalist than oriental. Lawrence and Anthea's main base is in Tangier, and whereas they have attempted – more or less successfully – to keep that apartment from becoming '*too Moorish*', their London *pied-à-terre* is dominated by a huge Moroccan lantern. Other such touches include a

24

three-piece suite originally made for the Belgian consul's house in Tangier, and a bouquet of tuberoses whose heady scent immediately evokes the Maghreb. 'We wanted this flat to be an antidote to the other one but ... even the colours ended up having a slight Tangier feel!' Mynott's portrait of the late expatriate David Herbert, a long-time Tangier resident, dominates the dining alcove, which vibrates to the planes of solid colour on the walls: fuchsia, Parma violet, olive, Hermès orange and vibrant green. 'We were attracted by the unusual volumes of the place, but our first concern was to break up the main room. It is thirty-two feet [nearly ten metres] long, and had been a shop, then an office, so it was particularly soulless. With the gold-leaf bookshelves and the slightly mad green and gold-leaf column acting as a divider, we managed to created two separate spaces. Then we painted the whole flat in a preposterous manner, in order to achieve a slightly constructivist effect of planes of contrasting colours. We discovered that the colours can be as bright and as different as you like, as long as you keep to the same intensity of tone ...' The Mynotts are not afraid of glorious statements in this mould – indeed, they thoroughly enjoy the visual shock their flat provides. Thus they entertain often, which they qualify as 'an artistic adventure more than pure *gourmandise*'. 'The great advantage of the flat is its central position – you can walk everywhere. People tend to think it's a bore living right in the middle of town – for shopping and things – but in fact there is a little street of shops just around the corner, where everyone knows everyone else – almost a village atmosphere. All ten minutes from Tottenham Court Road ...' The flat is vibrant – a heady mix of the pretty sublime and the ridiculously pretty: paper Christmas decorations do duty as table ornaments, flabbergastingly realistic fake orchids adorn side tables, and the prints on the wall are all Picassos. With their usual flair, the Mynotts have magicked up a charming home from an unprepossessing space by generous use of their combined, free-flowing imagination.

Anthea & Lawrence Mynott

On the previous pages: a portrait of the Mynotts in their ground-floor Bloomsbury flat. The detail is of a corner, lined with bookshelves, and given structure by a series of framed designs by Picasso for the *Ballet Russe* production of *La Tricorne*. *Opposite*: a view from the living area into the dining area giving the full force of the brilliantly contrasting colours – inspired by Sobranie cocktail cigarettes. *Above*: Lawrence Mynott's portrait of the late David Herbert, *doyen* of Tangier's expatriate set, and a Moroccan lantern evoke the Mynotts' North African home.

When, on Tom Dixon's cv, it says '1981–4 – Night-club promotion and event organization', it means the euphoria of being in your early twenties and having London buzzing about you; being part of the music scene, DJ-ing and running out-of-town 'raves' before the 'rave' was even invented. It speaks of Dixon's restlessness that eventually got him into designing furniture from bicycle handlebars, soup ladles and old frying pans. And that, because it was fun and corresponded to Dixon's boyish delight in 'making something out of nothing', became creative salvage, the neo-baroque movement, or the new 'English Eccentrics' design movement – arguably one of the most significant in the decorative arts of our *fin-de-siècle* epoch. In ten short years, Dixon has progressed from constructing chairs out of domestic debris to what he terms 'grown-up design'. 'I remember selling my first piece of scrap for £15 — and what amazed me was that someone would pay for it when it hadn't cost me anything to make. It appeared to be alchemy: turning nuts and bolts into gold.' As designing, 'although I have never really known what that word means —I tend to think

25

of myself more as a stylist, because I go for the good shapes, and if those shapes aren't functional it doesn't bother me', became his main activity, Dixon based himself on the All Saints Road, off Portobello. At that point it was 'very cost-effective, the classic place to get stabbed — and so scary no one would buy there'. The quirkiest of London's young creative elite were there, however: fashion designer Georgina Godley, French furniture designer André Dubreuil, and the set designers and camp icons Dean Bright and Pearl. It was a heady time, all the more brilliant for being much too short, and because the very protagonists were unaware of the wild successes that they were going to become. Nowadays, Dixon is the only one still faithful to the All Saints Road, which itself has become a little more respectable — much as he has. The maverick of cast iron and rusty metal has become a forward-looking entrepreneur. Dixon now works in plastic and aluminium, raffia and rattan when designing his light, airy and often colourful pieces, produced by the Japanese, by Capellini in Italy, or by his own label, Eurolounge. His pieces are part of the permanent collections of all the important museums world-wide who have an interest in design. More importantly, there are Dixons in all the best drawing rooms. His shop, Space, which opened on the All Saints Road in 1994, tried to some extent to recreate the workshop atmosphere of the early 1980s by encouraging and producing, as well as retailing the work of, a new generation of young British designers. Now the shop has been transferred to a more central location, and Dixon is moving back in. He will be living right next door to his very first workshop — altogether he has been involved in five buildings along the road. 'This is the first example of my own domestic architecture. The terrace of Victorian houses was so badly built that I felt I had the right to adapt it, and to make the interior something different. It had been badly designed to start off with, and then messily lived in — whatever I did had to be an improvement. I knew I could clean it up, and make it feel modern. I find it upsetting to live in a space that has no modernity about it ...' Dixon's flat is spread over three levels, the original ground floor and basement being connected by a room that he created by roofing over the yard. Although his two children and their mother, Claudia Nella, are used to living with the 'not necessarily functional' prototypes of Dixon pieces, there is also a sprinkling of eighteenth-century furniture inherited from his French grandmother, who lived in Tunisia where Dixon was born. 'Ideally I would not live with any of my own stuff — just 1960s and 1970s low-quality plastic and stretchy foamy bits ... but I do get bored and change everything every couple of months.' That, he adds, is the key to the evolutionary nature of his work, as well as to his home.

Claudia Nella &
Tom Dixon

On the previous pages: Tom and his children pictured perched on a distinctly unchildproof walkway above the main room. On page 171 there is a view of three of Tom's complimentary recent pieces. *Left*: the *Pylon* chair with the steel structure covered in velvety fabric designed for Capellini in 1991. The 'taco' lamps were designed by a colleague. *Opposite*: in the foreground, Dixon's famous *S* chair, also for Capellini; on the right his *Loop* bench in Philippine rattan, and another *Pylon* chair are placed around a prototype for a 1950s-inspired coffee table called *Spot*, also by Dixon.

The Chelsea house itself is remarkable, a monument to Arts-and-Crafts style. West House was built by Philip Webb for the Victorian watercolourist George Pryce Boyce, in 1869, shortly after building the Red House for William Morris. It became a centre for the Pre-Raphaelite Brotherhood, and Boyce wrote a definitive diary of their comings and goings. The man who inhabits the house now is one of the world's finest textile designers, a former professor of textiles at the Royal College of Art, with an intimate knowledge of British decorative arts throughout the ages. Bernard Nevill would have liked to have been born into the same generation as built West House. Today, it appears as a series of wonderful tableaux, almost like nineteenth-century watercolours, a little faded, but all the more sublime for their slightly unkempt feel. It reminds one of a rather grand, high-Victorian establishment, in which the master has an artistic bent, and the servants have been gladly neglecting their duties. It gives the impression of being full of heirlooms. In fact, Nevill bought almost every object himself in the late 1960s and early 1970s, 'great times for

26

bargains', replacing a houseful of similar, inherited furniture and paintings that he was forced to sell when an impoverished art student in the 1950s. The furnishings range from vast, English bookcases and sofas salvaged from the old Conservative Club, to beautifully battered Vuitton suitcases. The patina of time has had the happy effect of harmoniously allowing very different pieces to blend and cohabit. A collection of magnificent, antique textiles include many of William Morris' original Merton Abbey woven, wool curtains, still bearing the Morris & Co labels; Renaissance figurative tapestries; and bed hangings and covers of nineteenth-century lace. Nevill defines himself as an 'arranger' and indeed all the antique furniture, fabrics and decorative elements of disparate origins and eras work wonderfully together. Perhaps because he has 'eschewed the ordinary and the commonplace. I have an eye for grand pieces, with a bit of swagger'. Since the age of fourteen, he has been influenced by old volumes of *Country Life*, and dusty tomes that evoke the English stately home. All is, as the Victorians would have said, '… pleasing to the eye'. The drawing room overlooks the west-facing garden, and beyond that, the three-acre gardens of the Old Chelsea Rectory. The permanently unfinished state of West House is the result of the energy and time spent on Nevill's restoration of the remaining wing of Fonthill Abbey. The first Duke of Westminster built it to replace Wyatts Abbey, designed for the great eccentric connoisseur William Beckford. Fonthill is Nevill's country retreat, where he spends much of his time when not dealing with the grand French, German and Japanese companies he designs for. He also produces a collection of textiles and furniture under his own label with Hodsoll McKenzie Cloths, but he is probably best known as the man who brought Liberty fabrics back to life in the 1960s. His designs are often big and bold, but can also be gloriously subtle, jewel coloured and intricate. They reflect his impressive visual sophistication, much as does his London home.

Bernard Nevill

On the previous pages: a portrait of Bernard Nevill in his dark green breakfast room, and a detail of his luxuriant garden, with Edwardian cane and wicker 'dryad' chairs. *Above*: a partial view of the master bedroom through the dressing room showing, left, an Edwardian red silk damask screen behind a neo-Gothic oak table, and a corner of the fireplace. *Right*: a view of the landing, with its curtains in Morris 'Squirrel' woven wool fabric and the seventeenth-century sofa upholstered in Brussels tapestry. *Opposite*: a corner of the ante room, with its deliciously worn leather Chesterfield sofa. The portraits, and screen panels in Spanish leather, are seventeenth-century; the curtains are crewel work.

Above: a corner of the little sitting room, with the old leather sofa from the Conservative Club, and a collection of antique cushions; the walls are covered with nineteenth-century watercolours of English gardens by Helen Allingham, G. Elgood, Lillian Stannord and others. *Opposite*: the drawing room, with its oak and bronze bookcases salvaged from the Conservative Club. The large Ziegler carpet, heavy tapestry curtains, and the deep-seated Howard sofas give a quintessentially English atmosphere to the room. The library ladders were bought when *The Times* demolished its old building, and another, matching one turned up a few years later in a second-hand shop.

Opposite: the lace guest bedroom, showing part of Nevill's immense collection of antique lace. In this very feminine room, the watercolour over the dressing table is central to its composition. On the bed a Fortuny 'Delphos' dress and stamped velvet jacket from Bernard Nevill's collection of antique costumes. The screen on the left is upholstered in 'Briar Rose' by William Morris. The armchair by Rhulmann contrasts with the early nineteenth-century, deep-pile carpet. *Right and below*: two details of the lace bedroom, which overlooks the garden, give some idea of the impact created by this fabric when it is used with conviction.

Left: the tiled kitchen, with its classic, very English, scrubbed pine kitchen table, and a handsome array of antique copper pans evokes the Edwardian age; at the table stands a nineteenth-century, Gimson elm ladder chair. *Below*: a detail of the dining room, with its monumental, 1840 mahogany dining table and chairs; the billiard light was a bargain at £5 in 1967. Gascoigne's fifteen-foot-long (four-and-a-half-metre) *Turning the Plough* oil painting, which gives the room so much of its atmosphere, was shown at the Royal Academy in 1894. Hung on the main staircase of the Junior Carlton Club, it was bought for £7.10.

John Pawson, the ultimate architectural practician of London minimalism, once said that among all his clients Doris Lockhart Saatchi was the one who lived in the most appropriate way in the interiors he designed. 'Better, more minimally, in a way, than I do', he laughed. Architecturally, this is little short of being more Catholic than the pope. Living in a pared-down environment is an intimate compulsion for Saatchi, and she was Pawson's second client – after writer Bruce Chatwin. Her first commission was for a single room, an 'office and writing room', which she still remembers with delight. A few years later, she asked him to conceive the minmalist architecture of her mews house in Mayfair, which was entirely gutted and then rebuilt on three storeys. Minimalism always requires close attention to detail and careful finishing in order to be successful. By that time, Pawson's career had been well launched, and he was greatly in demand. Thus Saatchi found herself 'the project manager', which is perhaps why the house took six years to get exactly right, but may also be why she seems so perfectly at ease, so content in her white spaces. 'I'm really

27

happy here. It is truly serene. Here we are in the middle of a big, bustling, international city, but once past the door it is a peaceful place. Of course, that can be a danger too – the house sometimes seems hermetic, cut off from the outside world. It just becomes terribly tempting to stay in!' The finished project is effective because of the thoroughness of the concept; an essay in white walls, texture, light and volume. Such emptiness is indeed strangely seductive. With pleasure, Saatchi points out that her first-time dinner guests more often than not write impassioned thank-you letters to the effect that they have decided to throw out all their furniture … At Saatchi's there is not an awful lot of it. Although the first-floor drawing room boasts fine, vintage design pieces: a pair of Jean-Michel Frank white sofas, a caramel-leather day bed by Mies van der Rohe, and a pair of armchairs by Le Corbusier around a Knoll coffee table, they are all pieces of great purity, a reduction of function to its essence. On the ground floor, the only piece is a mahogany table that seats ten comfortably. 'I love to entertain, and have lots of people round, and for me the ideal dinner table is twelve feet long [three-and-half metres] … but we did not quite have the space.' Designed, like many other fittings in the house by Saatchi, with Pawson's then associate Claudio Silvestrin, the table is sculptural, with its supports made of the same *pietra serena* as the floors throughout. Around it are scattered a handful of chairs designed by Charles Eames in the 1950s. In the adjacent kitchen, screened from the dining room by an enormous panel of acid-etched glass, appliances – crockery, pots, pans and everything else – are stowed away behind Pawson's signature floor-to-ceiling cupboards. A long, T-shaped island block of stainless steel, 'like a Donald Judd sculpture', acts as breakfast counter, buffet table and generous work surface. For parties, the deep, square sink is filled with ice, and serves as ' a giant champagne bucket'. The daylight, which seeps in from a walled patio, and from behind white Venetian blinds, adds to the impression of time standing still, of distance from the bustle outside. As in Islamic architecture, the courtyard, inhabited only by a life-size nineteenth-century bronze Artemis, has the effect of concentrating all the energy of the house inwards. On the wall, the globes of Angela Bulloch's artwork *Daylight IV* pulsate on and off, contributing their own surreal effect. Following her involvement in the Saatchi Gallery, using white walls as a foil for adventurous modern art such as this was one of Saatchi's main points in her detailed brief to Pawson. 'I never wanted to make an architectural statement – the house is a backdrop for the art, for reading, working and entertaining. To my mind, minimalism is about making the constraints of structure disappear. It throws the people into relief.'

Doris Lockhart Saatchi

On the previous pages: a portrait of Doris Lockhart Saatchi by Michel Arnaud, and the ground-floor entrance corridor. *Above*: the kitchen, with its monolithic counter into which hob, sink, working and eating surfaces have been incorporated. In the background, a glimpse of the dining room; the 'rubber-gloves' work on the wall is by Craig Woods. *Right*: a general view of the dining room, whose table was designed by Saatchi and Silvestrin, and Charles Eames chairs produced by Vitra. The light sculpture is by Angela Bulloch, and glows on and off continuously; the bronze statue of Artemis in the courtyard was bought at a Sotheby's first sale of garden statuary.

Left: a view of the first-floor drawing room that occupies the entire breadth of the mews house. The sofas are Andrée Putman re-editions of a Jean-Michel Frank design – although Saatchi replaced the triple seat and the back cushions with single cushions. The painting to the left of the window is by Damien Hirst; the one on the right is a Sherrie Levine. *Below*: another view, showing the coffee table by Florence Knoll. The large diptych is by Gary Hume. The lamps are 1930s hospital lights, picked up in a Californian junk shop; Saatchi is so fond of them that she has four in her New York apartment too. *Opposite right*: a view of the curving stairwell created by Saatchi with Pawson and Silvestrin. *Opposite, bottom left*: the free-standing Carrara marble basin, designed by Saatchi and Silvestrin, is in all the bathrooms; the bedroom table (*opposite, bottom right*) is by Florence Knoll.

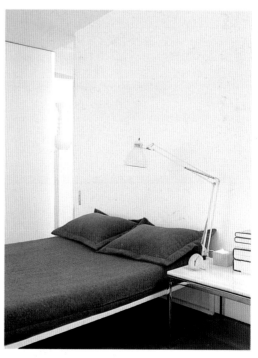

Visiting, as many do, Severs' 1724 home in Spitalfields, is an exercise in the suspension of disbelief. If, from the height of our late twentieth-century preoccupation with modernity, you can manage it, it is highly rewarding. Obsessive, and massively erudite, Severs holds the key to an emotional involvement with the past that is not often accessible. He lives in his home in much the same way that the Huguenot weavers may have done, each room — its furnishings, smells and decoration – corresponds to a specific period between the late seventeenth and early nineteenth centuries. There are several explanations for the existence of this 'time capsule' in Spitalfields. The more prosaic version is that Severs, repulsed by his native American 'fast-food' culture, used to 'close his eyes and think of England' while growing up in California. Upon his arrival in London in 1967, he immersed himself in the history of 'the old country'. He gave tours of London in a horse-drawn landau, stabled his horse in a condemned mews, and later, upon eviction, had his horse adopted by the queen and stabled at Buckingham Palace. This nostalgic process

culminated quite naturally in 1979 with the acquisition of this crumbling Georgian house. It had thankfully been spared the horrors of three centuries of 'improvements'. Its relatively authentic state — and the practical considerations of no electricity, heating or hot water — inspired him to live in it as the Georgians would have done, give or take the odd gaslight. He restored it on a shoestring, although its apparent opulence denies the fact. At this point, and because he had always looked into old paintings as though the frame was a window into the past, he decided to cross the metaphorical lintel, and created an imaginary family, the Jervises, remodelling the house around their invented lives over three centuries. They come alive to visitors, by candlelight, once a month. Severs then becomes stage manager, director, principal boy and alchemist, invoking the Jervises, and creating a heady atmosphere thick with the scent of cloves and candles, the hiss of the gas lamps, and the rich colours of the past. His grand old house becomes the setting for a brilliantly conceived 'still-life drama'. First come the sounds: a horse clip-clopping in the street, a servant girl at work upstairs, the voices of several men in the dining parlour to your right. His voice becomes urgent in your ears: 'Open the dining-parlour door and look. There it is: a scene – in three dimensions – at the heart of the reality which the sounds persuaded you to imagine. Its sitters have walked away, leaving behind only the material evidence of their presence. The old brass clock ticks and tocks, the candles are still alight, the fire still smoulders, and an evocative smell rushes out to invite you in.' Each step – don't bang your head — down the creaking stairs into the kitchen, 'straight out of *The Tailor of Gloucester*', with its blue-and-white china, and its *nature-morte* of sturdy nineteenth-century vegetables on the table, convinces you that this is more than stagecraft. A long way beyond the historical *son et lumière*, Severs is not simply a man of the theatre: he is a historian, and a fabulously talented stylist, obsessive about the emotional importance of the living homage to the past that he has created. A closer look at the furniture and finishes 'exposes the fact that though of good age, most things were originally collected for their charm, and are in disappointing condition'. Although obviously a born collector, Severs is not precious as to the details of historical accuracy: effect is all: the baroque moudlings in the hall are made of plastic fruit fused with the flame of a cigarette lighter, and then painted over several times. The important point is that each of the ten rooms works as an arrangement, as a visual tableau. The furniture — gathered from skips, markets and junk shops – are not meant to be the stars of the show. Severs and his imagination are.

Dennis Severs

On the previous pages: a view of Dennis Severs in his bed, which is not as grand as it looks, but was put together from Peter Jones remnants and a few planks. The exterior of the Huguenot weaver's house in Spitalfields stands out because of its red wooden shutters. *Left*: the gentleman's smoking room, in which the scene in Hogarth's painting *A Midnight Modern Conversation* of 1732, has been reproduced. This room relates to the mid-eighteenth century, and the years of maximum prosperity for the household. Another masculine room, *above* and detail *right*, refers to the first years of that century – it is the first room one comes to upon entering, and Puritanism and careful housekeeping are clearly in the air.

Left: a view of the basement kitchen, inspired by a Beatrix Potter drawing. This effect was added to by Severs having been able to pick up a bargain boxful of original blue-and-white Delft tiles. The dresser is loaded with an enormous collection of vintage crockery, all of which Severs uses in his day-to-day life. He does all his cooking on the wood-burning stove in the grate, and even in this dark room never relies on anything but candlelight. *Below*: a view of the landing, and its authentic-looking 1780s-style *epergne*. The creamware plates and baskets date from different periods, but they echo the decorative plasterwork on the staircases, which itself speaks evocatively of the flamboyance of the age.

Left: a view of Severs' massive, canopied bed, which is a true exercise in DIY. *Right*: the tableau of blue-and-white ceramic over the chimney breast in the bedroom; some are good, some are not, some are valuable, and some are modern tat, but the overall effect is that of an exuberant rococo room, well in keeping with the past history of the house. *On the following pages*: further views of this, the most theatrical room in the house, with its ornate hangings. The detailing is perfect, from the imaginary Mrs Jervis' dress, hanging from a screen, to the canary in its cage. At this point in the tour Severs points out that in this room 'the age of reason has been left behind, and a certain frivolity and grandeur is in the air'.

The initial sketch for Seth Stein's utterly surprising London home was done in the first half-hour of visiting the site. It took an architect as gifted and as daring as Stein to spot the potential in a singularly unprepossessing disused stable and builder's yard, partly overlooked by ugly new buildings. However, the odd site was in deepest Kensington, and thus highly desirable. Stein quickly decided that the two existing buildings that formed an L-shape could be supplemented by another L-shaped structure of his own design. This would create a low-slung rectangular house, with a central courtyard overlooked by the living areas and gallery. Having just returned from a trip to Japan, Stein could imagine the courtyard as both an Eastern haven of peace and the central element to his structure. 'It was all so perfectly clear to me: the house existed already in my imagination, and we ended up buying the land without planning permission. A risky move. Especially when we learnt that the land gave access to the London Underground tunnels, and thus had specific restrictions! The building had to be set back fourteen metres [about forty-six feet]

29

from the street because of that.' Once all the negotiating and paper-work were done, Stein launched himself into the project. Having set up on his own in the late 1980s, after working with some of the best contemporary architects in London, Stein was eager to make a bold statement, 'because it is so rare to have the space to do so'. Today, the house is quite magical; splashed with vibrant pink and indigo in an otherwise undefiled powder white, it seems to belong more to California or Mexico than to Kensington. At the centre of the structure lies the 'Zen' garden; another innovative notion, as the 'courtyard house' is itself an architectural blueprint hardly ever seen in London. Indeed, much of the house's initial capacity to surprise and delight comes from its being a completely new departure for British domestic architecture. One of its other unexpected qualities is that despite Stein being particularly articulate about his influences and desires, the finished house appeals to the senses rather than to the mind. The conception may have been principally cerebral, but the end result is thoroughly sensual, which is not a word that one usually associates with minimalism. Stein's iconoclastic design includes large spaces, bold washes of colour, organic shapes and myriad textures, from polished cement through frosted glass, to wood and ceramics. This adds to its tactile and visual richness. As twilight falls, it becomes apparent that the lighting has also been thought out with an elaborate thoroughness. From one side of the house to the other, through glass doors and huge windows, the other rooms are apparent, like a careful sequence of minimalist stage sets. The vivid colours of a few, carefully selected pieces of modern design stand out against the white. The frosted façade glows pinkly, due to the Matisse-coloured wall behind it, looking excitingly odd from the street. Inside, the touches of vibrant colour really come into their own with careful lighting adding to the house's graphic impact. Stein has studied every angle, every effect. It is almost a relief to find that the 'chandelier' in the dining room consists of a bundle of bunched-up fairy lights. And that the piece on the wall is not art with a capital 'A', but simply the remains of the tiled stable wall, with all the horses' numbers still stencilled on it. 'It is', says Stein, 'the rebirth of what was here.'

Seth Stein

On the previous pages: a portrait of Seth Stein in the doorway of his Kensington home and the detail shows a free-standing concrete cylinder which contains the cloakroom. At night, the sandblasted glass panel and clever lighting diffuse the pink glow of the wall behind, evoking the paintings of Rothko, or of English artist Michael Craig Martin. The façade epitomizes the 'effect of an abstract combination of colours and shapes' that Stein was seeking to create. *Above*: a nocturnal view, taken from the lawn in the courtyard that the house is built around. The glass walls are the membrane that creates a distinction between inside and out, without creating a visual boundary. *Right*: the view from the opposite direction.

Left: the view from the living room through the sliding-glass door, framed in orange-enamelled steel. The courtyard was conceived with a Japanese garden in mind. At night, the most intriguing visual focusing point is a luminous square on the far wall – the pink paint of the far corridor glimpsed through a cleverly placed window. The terracotta pot is Italian. Spanish limestone stairs lead up to the roof terrace, where the curved, concrete gazebo for summer dining is only just visible. *Above*: a view of the kitchen, with its high, simple, white bar that conceals all the equipment and fittings. The chairs are by Arne Jacobsen, the table, designed by Eero Saarinen, has been adapted by Seth Stein by polishing the aluminium base and fitting a maple-wood top.

Left: a daylight view of the façade revealing the graphic quality of the composition – almost cubist. The effect of the bands of shade from the canopy add to the impression. The daytime views include the sweeping and expressive stairway that Stein designed to lead up to the bedrooms and bathrooms. The chair is by Marc Newson, from David Gill and echoes the sensual lines of the staircase. *Above right*: another view from the glass-walled gallery that illustrates the effective visual contrast between the very graphic lines of the structural architecture and the surprising sweep of the stairway. The canvas to the right is *Compression No 7* by Mark Francis.

'The only thing that really worried me was that it meant living above the office', reminisces architect John Young, while lesser souls would have quailed at the sheer intrepidity required to build and live in this vast glass eyrie on the Thames. Young, however, maintains that the whole apartment was 'reaction to domestic clutter', and that its very emptiness is soothing, as 'all personal property can be stowed away, and the architecture can be left to speak for itself'. The long-time partner of Richard Rogers, over the years Young has magicked the most fantastically abstract concepts behind the controversial Lloyds' Building into reality. His own apartment, built in 1989 atop the famous Rogers-designed block of riverside apartments in Hammersmith, shows Young at his uncompromising best. He is wedded to the techniques of industrial craftsmen; fanatical about things like alloys, tempered steel, plate-coil discs, and all the myriad possibilities for adapting industrial techniques and finishes to the domestic interior. He is also a virtuoso of the grand gesture: floor-to-ceiling glass walls, vast, empty rooms, towers and turrets, aerial steel

30

gangplanks, a bed on four thin steel rods on a platform that hangs from the soaring ceiling ... The apartment is really only one enormous, flowing space hanging above the sweep of the river, cradled by the elements. Young describes his work as 'a richness of dimension, floating volumes ... and a bit of whimsy'. It is very impressive, especially when it rains at Thames Wharf, and you feel yourself poised in mid-air as if in a glass-and-concrete pod, suspended among the raindrops. This effect is even more striking in the tiny, curved, glass conservatory on the roof that evokes a lighthouse's chamber, and from which the view is singularly impressive — if you can brave the high-tech gangplank that leads up there! 'Since we moved in, I haven't stopped tweaking — it's like a never-ending hobby. I change door knobs, work on perfecting the heating system, think about installing electronic blinds ...' The one disadvantage that Young admits to is that 'it is rarely uncomfortably hot'. This seems fairly understandable, as his rather beautiful plate-coil heaters (specially welded in Texas) that adorn the walls have an awful lot of glass walls for which to compensate. The bathroom, for example, situated in its very own circular tower constructed entirely of glass bricks, also has a clear glass roof. 'I was very influenced by a trip to Japan — the whole ceremonial of the

bathing ritual. So I put in a cedar-wood tub and thought that one would be able to gaze up at the stars from it. The whole house is about capturing that beautiful quality of life.' Contrary to appearances — precision constructions in steel and concrete rarely evoke such feelings — Young's architecture is deeply romantic. Romantic, because it questions orthodox ideas about space with such passion, and because it is lived in with the same conviction.

John Young

On pages 208-9: a portrait of John Young and a detail of the glass walls of his extraordinary apartment. *On pages 210-11*: a view of the main space, illustrating the interplay between the view and the apartment, with its double-height windows. The floors are of waxed concrete, and the walls of polished plaster throughout. The round metal fixtures on the wall are industrial plate-coil heaters, that in this new context appear as sophisticated as the classic Le Corbusier armchairs or Ward Bennett dining tables. *Below*: the impressive, mobile, stainless-steel cupboards, behind which all the clutter of daily life is stowed. *Right*: not the galley of a state-of-the-art submarine, but the kitchen, finished in similarly industrial materials.

Left: the spectacular glass-brick bathroom. It is circular, and occupies its own tower, with the cedar-wood Japanese sunken tub positioned in the centre. The rest of the bathroom fittings are of stainless steel. The bathroom is the highest room in the building, although Young has built a rooftop observatory that echoes its circular shape. The spiral staircase that can be seen to the extreme right of the image is the external stairs leading to the second roof terrace where the observatory is situated.

ACKNOWLEDGEMENTS

This book would not have been possible without my friend and advisor, Anna Davenport, who contributed greatly to this project.

The support of Tiggy Maconochie, Ed Victor, Carol Ryan and my agent, Maggie Phillips, was invaluable.

Also a big thank you to Elizabeth Kime, Christopher Gibbs, and Karen Howes at the Interior Archive, Lynne Bryant at Arcaid, Sue Bartlett at Elizabeth Whiting & Associates, Ulli Weber, Doris Saatchi, Ricardo Cinalli, Ian Dew and Alison Martin, Nick Knight, Roland Beaufre, Henry Wilson, Gillian Cargill, Ray Main, Martyn Thompson, Peter Copestake, Derry Moore and Snowdon.

This book is dedicated to Nicolas.

BIBLIOGRAPHY

THE LOOK OF LONDON

The Elements of Style. An Encyclopedia of Domestic Architectural Detail, General Editor: Stephen Calloway (Mitchell Beazley, 1991)

Georgian London, J Summerson (Pimlico, 1991)

London the Unique City, Steen Eiler Rasmussen (Penguin, 1934)

London Minimum, Herbert Ypma (Thames & Hudson, 1996)

The Story of Architecture, P. Nuttgens (Phaidon, 1993)

GENERAL

Change at King's Cross, Michael Hunter and Robert Thorne (Historical Publications, 1990)

Craigie, The Art of Craigie Aitchison, Andrew Gibbon Williams (Canongate Books, 1996)

The Faber Book of London, edited by A. N. Wilson (Faber and Faber, 1994)

Georgian London, John Summerson (Pimlico, 1991)

Gilbert and George, Galleria d'Arte Moderna, Bologna (Charta, 1996)

Gilbert and George, China Exhibition, National Art Gallery (Peking, 1993)

Langlands & Bell, Adrian Dannatt (Catalogue: Campana, Frankfurt; Moncada, Rome; Paley, London)

Life in the Georgian City, Dan Cruickshank and Neil Burton (Viking, 1990)

Ricardo Cinalli, John Russell Taylor (Edizioni della Bezuga, 1992)

Tom Dixon, Photographs by Cindy Palmano, Essay by Michael Collins (Architecture Design and Technology Press, 1990)

The Saving of Spitalfields, Marc Girouard and others (Spitalfields Historic Buildings Trust, 1989)